Linguistic Evidence for the Northern Origin
of Selected Psalms

THE SOCIETY OF BIBLICAL LITERATURE
MONOGRAPH SERIES

Adela Yarbro Collins, Editor
E.F. Campbell, Associate Editor

Number 43
LINGUISTIC EVIDENCE FOR THE NORTHERN
ORIGIN OF SELECTED PSALMS

by
Gary A. Rendsburg

Gary A. Rendsburg

LINGUISTIC EVIDENCE
FOR THE NORTHERN ORIGIN
OF SELECTED PSALMS

Scholars Press
Atlanta, Georgia

LINGUISTIC EVIDENCE FOR THE NORTHERN ORIGIN
OF SELECTED PSALMS

by
Gary A. Rendsburg

Library of Congress Cataloging in Publication Data

Rendsburg, Gary.
    Linguistic evidence for the northern origin of selected Psalms /
    Gary A. Rendsburg.
    p. cm. -- (Monograph series / The Society of Biblical
    Literature ; no. 43)
    Includes bibliographical references and indexes.
    ISBN 1-55540-565-7 (alk. paper). -- ISBN 1-55540-566-5 (pbk. :
    alk. paper)
    1. Bible. O.T. Psalms--Language, style. 2. Bible. O.T.
Psalms--Criticism, interpretation, etc. 3. Hebrew language-
-Dialects. I. Title. II. Title: Northern origin of selected
Psalms. III. Series: Monograph series (Society of Biblical
Literature) ; no. 43)
BS1430.5.R46 1990
223'.2066--dc20   90-19926
                                           CIP

Printed in the United States of America
on acid-free paper

To my parents
Julius and Irene Rendsburg

TABLE OF CONTENTS

ABBREVIATIONS

AB   Anchor Bible

AJSL   *American Journal of Semitic Languages and Literatures*

ANET   J. B. Pritchard, *Ancient Near Eastern Texts Relating to the Old Testament* (Princeton: Princeton University Press, 1969)

AnOr   Analecta Orientalia

AOAT   Alter Orient und Altes Testament

AOS   American Oriental Series

ASTI   *Annual of the Swedish Theological Institute*

BASOR   *Bulletin of the American Schools of Oriental Research*

BASORSS   Bulletin of the American Schools of Oriental Research Supplementary Studies

BASP   *Bulletin of the American Society of Papyrologists*

BASS   *Beiträge zur Assyriologie und semitschen Sprachwissenschaft*

BDB   F. Brown, S. R. Driver, and C. A. Briggs, *A Hebrew and English Lexicon of the Old Testament* (Oxford: Clarendon Press, 1906)

BH   Biblical Hebrew

BHS   *Biblia Hebraica Stuttgartensia*, eds. K. Elliger and W. Rudolph (Stuttgart: Deutsche Bibelstiftung, 1977)

BZ   *Biblische Zeitschrift*

BZAW   Beihefte zur Zeitschrift für die alttestamentliche Wissenschaft

CBQ   *Catholic Biblical Quarterly*

EBH   Early Biblical Hebrew

EM	*Enṣiqlopediya Miqraʾit*, 8 vols. (Jerusalem: Mosad Bialik, 1950–82)
GKC	E. Kautzsch, *Gesenius' Hebrew Grammar*, trans. A. E. Cowley (Oxford: Clarendon Press, 1910)
HAR	*Hebrew Annual Review*
HKAT	Handkommentar zum Alten Testament
HSM	Harvard Semitic Monographs
HTR	*Harvard Theological Review*
HUCA	*Hebrew Union College Annual*
ICC	International Critical Commentary
IEJ	*Israel Exploration Journal*
IH	Israelian Hebrew
IOS	*Israel Oriental Studies*
JANES	*Journal of the Ancient Near Eastern Society*
JAOS	*Journal of the American Oriental Society*
JBL	*Journal of Biblical Literature*
JBLMS	Journal of Biblical Literature Monograph Series
JH	Judahite Hebrew
JJPES	*Journal of the Jewish Palestine Exploration Society*
JJS	*Journal of Jewish Studies*
JNES	*Journal of Near Eastern Studies*
JNSL	*Journal of Northwest Semitic Languages*
JQR	*Jewish Quarterly Review*
JPOS	*Journal of the Palestine Oriental Society*
JPSV	Jewish Publication Society Version
JRAS	*Journal of the Royal Asiatic Society*
JSOTSS	Journal for the Study of the Old Testament Supplement Series
JSS	*Journal of Semitic Studies*
JTS	*Journal of Theological Studies*
KB	L. Koehler and W. Baumgartner, *Lexicon in Veteris Testamenti libros* (Leiden: E. J. Brill, 1953)
LBH	Late Biblical Hebrew
MH	Mishnaic Hebrew
MT	Masoretic Text

NT	*Novum Testamentum*
OBO	Orbis Biblicus et Orientalis
OTL	Old Testament Library
OTS	*Oudtestamentische Studiën*
PEQ	*Palestine Exploration Quarterly*
PJB	*Palästinajahrbuch*
RB	*Revue Biblique*
RBI	*Rivista Biblica Italiana*
SBH	Standard Biblical Hebrew
SBLDS	Society of Biblical Literature Dissertation Series
SVT	Supplements to Vetus Testamentum
TLZ	*Theologische Literaturzeitung*
UBL	Ugaritisch-biblische Literatur
UF	*Ugarit-Forschungen*
UT	C. H. Gordon, *Ugaritic Textbook* (AnOr 38; Rome: Pontifical Biblical Institute, 1967)
VT	*Vetus Testamentum*
WO	*Die Welt des Orients*
ZAW	*Zeitschrift für die alttestamentliche Wissenschaft*
ZDMG	*Zeitschrift der deutschen morgenländischen Gesellschaft*
ZKT	*Zeitschrift für katholische Theologie*

PREFACE

This book developed out of research conducted at the Hebrew University in Jerusalem in 1987. It is my pleasant duty to thank the National Endowment for the Humanities for its Fellowship for College Teachers which enabled me to pursue my research in Israel. The staffs of the Hebrew University, the Jewish National and University Library, and the École Biblique were always congenial and helpful.

I profited greatly from discussions with two members of the Hebrew University faculty, namely, Avi Hurvitz and Shelomo Morag. They acted as a sounding board for many of the ideas set forth in this monograph, and guided me with good counsel on a variety of issues.

I am also grateful to Edward F. Campbell and Adela Yarbro Collins for accepting this volume in the Society of Biblical Literature Monograph Series. As an editor myself, I am especially appreciative of Professor Campbell's careful eye and efficient manner. W. Randall Garr and Richard J. Clifford served as readers for the book. I am indebted to these two scholars for their helpful comments and for many suggestions which were incorporated into the book's final version.

On the technical side, thanks are due to Marty Klionsky for drawing the hieroglyphs which adorn the dedication page; to my students Richard Dietrich and Richard Wright (the former produced the indexes and proofread the work, the latter produced the bibliography); and to my friends Richard and Nancy Freimark, who allowed me continued access to their laser printer.

Finally, I dedicate this book to my parents, Julius and Irene Rendsburg. It was in their house as a child that I first learned to love language, to appreciate bilingualism, and to recognize dialectal variation. For this, and for everything else, I express my love.

INTRODUCTION

The Strata of Biblical Hebrew

Several generations of biblical scholars have grown up with the false notion of "the harmonizing activity of the Masoretes."[1] Such an understanding has led scholars to believe that the language of the Hebrew Bible is a unified whole with little dialectal variation. Upon closer inspection, however, it becomes obvious that this is not the case. On the contrary, it has become ever and ever clearer that the Masoretes simply transmitted what they had received and that no harmonization process ever occurred. The result is that Biblical Hebrew (BH) incorporates different strata which can be isolated through a close study of the grammar and lexicon of the language.

One such variation is chronological. Already in the 19th Century scholars began to isolate forms and words which they believed were representative of Late Biblical Hebrew (LBH) in contrast to Standard Biblical Hebrew (SBH).[2] Major work in this area in more recent years has been accomplished by A. Hurvitz. In several dozen studies he has shown beyond doubt that a chronological development may be seen in BH,[3] with the Exile of 586–538 B.C.E. representing a watershed between SBH and LBH.

Similarly, other scholars have worked towards isolating features of the language which may be classified as Early Biblical Hebrew (EBH). Perhaps not unexpectedly, this approach has been especially

---

[1] E. Kautzsch in GKC, vii. For an almost verbatim comment, see G. R. Driver, "Hebrew Studies," *JRAS* (1948) 175.

[2] Numerous examples are referred to in S. R. Driver, *An Introduction to the Literature of the Old Testament* (New York: Charles Scribner's Sons, 1906); and in BDB.

[3] The two monographs are A. Hurvitz, *Beyn Lashon le-Lashon* (Jerusalem: Bialik, 1972); and A. Hurvitz, *A Linguistic Study of the Relationship Between the Priestly Source and the Book of Ezekiel* (Paris: J. Gabalda, 1982). For a recent listing of his articles see pp. xiii–xiv in the latter book.

successful in dating biblical poetry. Here I will mention only the oft-cited article of W. L. Moran[4] and an important monograph by D. A. Robertson.[5] In this endeavor the Canaanite glosses of the Amarna letters have been especially helpful.[6]

These and related studies have led scholars in recent years to cease viewing BH as a monolithic structure. Instead, Hebraists often now speak of BH as a tripartite structure, to be divided diachronically into EBH, SBH, and LBH. The posthumously published synthesis by E. Y. Kutscher is a prime example of this approach.[7]

The heterogeneous nature of BH can also be seen synchronically, in fact in several such ways. Although it is clear that BH is essentially a literary language, scholars must also contend with the phenomenon of diglossia. As originally defined by C. A. Ferguson, diglossia refers to two co-existing varieties of the same language, one used for literary and formal purposes and one used for colloquial and informal purposes.[8]

By all accounts, BH represents the former.[9] But there can be no doubt that spoken Hebrew differed considerably from the BH norm;[10]

---

[4] W. L. Moran, "The Hebrew Language in its Northwest Semitic Background," in *The Bible and the Ancient Near East: Essays in Honor of William Foxwell Albright* (ed. G. E. Wright; Garden City, NY: Doubleday, 1961) 54–72. Although Moran's article treats all of BH, a disproportionate number of the examples he cites are from biblical poetry.

[5] D. A. Robertson, *Linguistic Evidence in Dating Early Hebrew Poetry* (SBLDS 3; Missoula, MT: Society of Biblical Literature, 1972).

[6] The scholar may now benefit from the excellent collection of all the relevant material in D. Sivan, *Grammatical Analysis and Glossary of the Northwest Semitic Vocables in Akkadian Texts of the 15th–13th C. B.C. from Canaan and Syria* (AOAT 214; Neukirchen-Vluyn: Neukirchener Verlag, 1984). In addition to the Amarna material, this volume collects the evidence from Ugarit, Taanach, and Alalakh.

[7] E. Y. Kutscher, *A History of the Hebrew Language* (Jerusalem: Magnes, 1982) 12, 77–85. Kutscher used the term Archaic Biblical Hebrew, whereas I prefer the label EBH.

[8] C. A. Ferguson, "Diglossia," *Word* 15 (1959) 325–340. The term diglossia has come to mean different things to different people in the past thirty years; see J. A. Fishman, "The Sociology of Language," in *Current Trends in Linguistics* (14 vols.; ed. T. A. Sebeok; The Hague: Mouton, 1963–76) 12.1689–1701; and J. A. Fishman, "Bilingualism With and Without Diglossia; Diglossia With and Without Bilingualism," *Journal of Social Issues* 23 (1967) 29–38. As I use the word herein, I have in mind Ferguson's original concept.

[9] J. Blau (*A Grammar of Biblical Hebrew* [Wiesbaden: Otto Harrassowitz, 1976] 1) has succinctly stated this in describing BH as "always a *literary* language" (italics his).

[10] See W. Chomsky, *Hebrew: The Eternal Language* (Philadelphia: Jewish Publication Society, 1964) 161.

indeed probably it was much closer to Mishnaic Hebrew (MH).[11] Proof of this is forthcoming from the literally hundreds of non-standard BH forms which anticipate MH. I have collected this evidence in my recent book on the subject,[12] and in many ways I was preceded by the work of A. Bendavid.[13] In short, these departures from the norms of BH grammar fully attest the inadequacy of the aforementioned view concerning the work of the Masoretes.

Another recent development in the field of Hebrew studies is the discovery of style-switching or code-switching. S. A. Kaufman has noted that in a number of famous instances the speech of Transjordanians is tinged with unusual grammatical forms and rare lexical items, many of which are typically classified as Aramaisms.[14] He is undoubtedly correct that in these texts "we have not to do with late language or foreign authors, but rather with the intentional stylistic representations of Trans-Jordanian speech on the part of Hebrew authors within Hebrew texts."[15] This approach to the biblical text is only just developing,[16] but again it points to the fact that the Masoretic Text (MT) has preserved a great variety of dialectal differences within the relatively large corpus of the Bible.

Finally, we come to the issue which will be the focus of our study: regional variation. The vast majority of biblical literature undoubtedly was composed in Judah in general or in Jerusalem in particular or by exiles from Judah and Jerusalem. Accordingly, the regional

---

[11] This has been emphasized by M. H. Segal, *A Grammar of Mishnaic Hebrew* (Oxford: Clarendon Press, 1927) 11; and E. Ullendorff, *Is Biblical Hebrew a Language?* (Wiesbaden: Otto Harrassowitz, 1977) 11.

[12] G. A. Rendsburg, *Diglossia in Ancient Hebrew* (AOS; Ann Arbor, MI: American Oriental Society, 1990).

[13] A. Bendavid, *Leshon ha-Miqraʾ u-Lshon Ḥakhamim* (2 vols.; Tel Aviv: Dvir, 1967–71).

[14] Similar techniques are well-known from other literatures. See, e.g., F. C. Robinson, "Some Aspects of the *Maldon* Poet's Artistry," *Journal of English and Germanic Philology* 75 (1976) 25–28, who discusses Scandinavicisms in the speech of the Vikings in the Old English poem "The Battle of Maldon." I am indebted to my former student Ann Crook for bringing this example and this article to my attention.

[15] S. A. Kaufman, "The Classification of the North West Semitic Dialects of the Biblical Period and Some Implications Thereof," in *Proceedings of the Ninth World Congress of Jewish Studies* (Panel Sessions: Hebrew and Aramaic Languages; Jerusalem: World Union of Jewish Studies, 1988) 54–55.

[16] For another example see J. C. Greenfield, "Aramaic Studies and the Bible," in *Congress Volume Vienna 1980* (ed. J. A. Emerton; SVT 32; Leiden: E. J. Brill, 1981) 129–30. For a brief, earlier statement, see N. H. Tur-Sinai, "ʾAramit: Hashpaʿat ha-ʾAramit ʿal ha-ʿIvrit shel ha-Miqraʾ," *EM* 1 (1965) 593–94.

standard of the Bible may be called Judahite Hebrew (JH). But stories which emanate from the north, such as those concerning the northern judges or the northern kings, often reflect different grammatical usages. These divergences are to be attributed to a northern Hebrew dialect, which I propose to call Israelian Hebrew (IH).[17] By Israelian I mean all portions of ancient Israel which lay within the boundaries of the northern kingdom, thus incorporating everything from approximately Bethel northward in Cisjordan and all of Transjordan. Or to put it in negative terms, everything which is not Judahite should be termed Israelian.[18]

The present monograph is devoted to the book of Psalms. Although linguistic investigation into the Psalms has been a popular topic in the recent past,[19] and although scholars commonly have suggested that a particular psalm here or there is northern in origin,[20] these two approaches have not been combined. That is to say, an inquiry into whether or not a particular hypothesized northern psalm contains features of IH has not been attempted. Accordingly, the time seems ripe to conduct such a study.

---

[17] I have coined this term based on the usage of H. L. Ginsberg, *The Israelian Heritage of Judaism* (New York: Jewish Theological Seminary, 1982). It is gratifying to see that S. Gevirtz ("Of Syntax and Style in the 'Late Biblical Hebrew'—'Old Canaanite' Connection," *JANES* 18 [1986] 25 and n. 1) independently adduced the same term.

[18] The territory of Benjamin is the border region. One would expect that its political union with Judah from c. 930 to 586 shaped its dialect in a Judahite manner. On the other hand, there is no *a priori* reason to assume that the same variety of Hebrew was spoken in Benjamin and in Judah. In modern Israel, for example, trained speakers of colloquial Arabic can often pinpoint the locale of a particular speaker to his village. In Great Britain this is a popular sport as well, and the Henry Higgins character of George Bernard Shaw fame is not as great an exaggeration as it may seem. The language of the stories in 1 Samuel concerned with Saul (which may be presumed to have been composed in Benjamin) may confirm our assumption, since IH elements may be found therein. Similarly, I believe that many of the peculiarities in the language of Jeremiah, the prophet from Anathoth, may be explained as IH features. See the numerous examples from 1 Samuel and Jeremiah collected in G. A. Rendsburg, "Morphological Evidence for Regional Dialects in Ancient Hebrew," in *Linguistics and Biblical Hebrew* (ed. W. Bodine; Winona Lake, IN: Eisenbrauns, forthcoming).

[19] See M. Tsevat, *A Study of the Language of the Biblical Psalms* (JBLMS 9; Philadelphia: Society of Biblical Literature, 1955); Hurvitz, *Beyn Lashon le-Lashon*; and Robertson, *Linguistic Evidence*.

[20] For examples, see below.

Israelian Hebrew

The immediate question which needs to be answered is how does one isolate an IH feature in particular or an IH text in general. We shall deal first with the finer issue of isolating grammatical elements of IH, and then turn to the larger issue of isolating IH compositions below. The biblical scholar today is blessed with an ever-growing corpus of Northwest Semitic inscriptions roughly contemporary with the biblical period. Many of these have in fact been found either within the territorial boundaries of the northern kingdom of Israel, or within close proximity to this area.

The languages or dialects of these inscriptions which are germane to us are Phoenician, Moabite, Ammonite, Aramaic, and the language of the Deir ʿAlla Balaam texts. Now, a comparison of these texts with the biblical corpus has yielded the finding that many of the standard features of the former appear in the latter only irregularly. Well known examples are the masculine plural nominal ending -*yn* (Moabite, Deir ʿAlla, Aramaic), the relative pronouns *z(y)* and (ʾ)*š* (Phoenician, Aramaic, Ammonite), and the feminine singular demonstrative pronoun *z*(ʾ) (Phoenician, Aramaic), but in truth there are many others.[21]

The dictates of dialect geography teach us that it is most likely for such forms to appear in Hebrew in the regions bordering the Phoenician, Moabite, Ammonite, Aramaic, and Deir ʿAlla speech-communities.[22] This is not to say that a particular Aramaic form could not have wound its way to Judah, for obviously the intelligentsia of Jerusalem could read, write, speak, and comprehend Aramaic (see 2 Kgs 18:26 = Isa 36:11). But all things being equal, we will assume that parallels of the sort mentioned above were characteristic of a Hebrew dialect or of Hebrew dialects spoken and written in northern Israel.

In more precise terms, I assume that the Hebrew of Asher, Zebulun, and Naphtali was closer to Phoenician, the Hebrew of Reuben was closer to Moabite,[23] the Hebrew of Gad was closer to Ammonite

---

[21] Happily, the scholar's task has been made much easier by the appearance of the comprehensive and exceedingly useful volume by W. R. Garr, *Dialect Geography of Syria-Palestine. 1000–586 B.C.E.* (Philadelphia: University of Pennsylvania Press, 1985).

[22] For a clear presentation of the methods of dialect geography, see J. K. Chambers and P. Trudgill, *Dialectology* (Cambridge: Cambridge University Press, 1980) 15–36, 103–24.

[23] In several instances in this book, I adduce Moabite material as evidence for a particular linguistic trait being characteristic of northern Hebrew. I am well aware, naturally, that Moab lies on the same latitude as Judah. However, insofar

and Deir ʿAlla,[24] and the Hebrew of Dan, Issachar, and eastern Manasseh was closer to Aramaic,[25] than any of these regional varieties was to JH.

Linguistics is not our only guide here. Historical considerations are also important. To take the example of the postulated similarity between the Hebrew of Dan, Issachar, and eastern Manasseh and the neighboring Aramaic, it should be mentioned that contacts between Israel and Aram were always strong.[26] These contacts undoubtedly led to the dialects of Aram and of northern Israel sharing a number of grammatical and lexical features. It is important to note that a one-word Aramaic inscription *lṭ[b]hy*ʾ "for the cooks" from the 9th Century B.C.E. has been found at Tel Dan, and that another one-word Aramaic inscription *lšqy*ʾ "for the cupbearers" from the 9th Century B.C.E. was uncovered at Ein Gev.[27] Similarly, contacts between coastal

---

as it borders the northern kingdom of Israel, specifically the territory of Reuben, we can assume more links between Moabite and IH than between Moabite and JH. Furthermore, the analysis of Garr, *Dialect Geography*, 229–31, demonstrates that among the Canaanite dialects only Deir ʿAlla was closer to Aramaic than Moabite. Consequently, there should be no objection to utilizing Moabite as a source for the reconstruction of IH.

[24] For an example of a phonological trait shared by Gileadite (= Gadite) Hebrew and Ammonite, see G. A. Rendsburg, "The Ammonite Phoneme /Ṯ/," BASOR 269 (1988) 73–79; and G. A. Rendsburg, "More on Hebrew *Šibbōlet*," JSS 33 (1988) 255–58.

[25] When citing Aramaic in this book, I have used the inscriptional Aramaic evidence whenever possible. However, due to the limited nature of this material, I have also cited evidence from later dialects, such as Biblical Aramaic, Targumic Aramaic, Talmudic Aramaic, and Syriac. I assume that if we possessed more Old Aramaic texts, many of the lexemes and forms which appear only in later dialects would occur in the early material also. This approach underlies almost all works dealing with language contact between Hebrew and Aramaic (e.g., M. Wagner, *Die lexikalischen und grammatikalischen Aramaismen im alttestamentlichen Hebräisch* (BZAW 96; Berlin: A. Töpelman, 1966).

[26] For discussion see W. T. Pitard, *Ancient Damascus* (Winona Lake, IN: Eisenbrauns, 1987).

[27] For quick reference see R. Hestrin, *et al.*, *Ketubot Mesaprot* (Jerusalem: Israel Museum, 1973) 129–30. I am indebted to Avi Hurvitz for bringing this epigraphic evidence to my attention. For the original publications see N. Avigad, "An Inscribed Bowl from Dan," *PEQ* 100 (1968) 42–44; and B. Mazar, A. Biran, M. Dothan, and I. Dunayevsky, "ʿEin Gev Excavations in 1961," *IEJ* 14 (1964) 27–29. Avigad claimed that "the Aramaic language of the inscriptions points to an Aramaean occupation of both places" (p. 44) and he cited 1 Kgs 15:20 = 2 Chr 16:4 as proof of this. However, even without Aramean occupation of the region, I assume that IH and Aramaic had much in common.

Phoenicia and inland Galilee were always strong and this no doubt helped cement the relationship between Phoenician and IH.[28]

In the above list of affinities between the tribal dialects and neighboring languages, I have omitted Ephraim and western Manasseh. The reason is obvious: this region did not border directly on any foreign area. At first glance, this would seem to be an important omission. Since the capital cities of the northern kingdom were located in Ephraim and western Manasseh, most Israelian literature probably emanated from this region. But even in these tribes we know that the Hebrew was in some regards closer to Moabite and Phoenician. I refer, of course, to the Samaria ostraca, which inform us that monophthongization of *aw/ay* was more complete in Samaria than it was in Judah, and that *št* "year" linked this dialect with Moabite and Phoenician as opposed to JH.[29]

A special word needs to be said now about Ugaritic. The evidence of this language must be carefully weighed because of the unique relationship between Ugaritic and BH. Vis-à-vis the latter, the former is both a northern language and a language attested several centuries earlier. Accordingly, it cannot be determined with certainty whether differences between Ugaritic and BH are due to variations in space or in time. Ginsberg, however, has garnered a considerable amount of evidence to justify gathering Ugaritic and Phoenician into a "Phoenic group" of dialects as distinct from a "Hebraic group" within the Northwest Semitic sphere.[30] In light of this analysis, it seems reasonable to utilize the Ugaritic material to establish connections specifically between IH and languages used to the north of Israel.

The same considerations hold in utilizing the evidence of the Amarna letters for our study. Obviously, a feature which appears in the Amarna letters which emanated from Jerusalem cannot be used to isolate IH features. However, since the vast majority of the Amarna letters stems from Byblos, Tyre, and other northern sites, generally the material is appropriate for our purposes. Therefore, occasionally in this study we will cite Amarna evidence to support our effort toward the reconstruction of IH.

---

[28] For the relationship between Phoenicia and northern Israel, see R. S. Hanson, *Tyrian Influence in the Upper Galilee* (Cambridge, MA: American Schools of Oriental Research, 1980). This volume deals mainly with the Persian and Hellenistic periods, but obviously the conclusions reached by Hanson hold equally for the earlier period.

[29] Garr, *Dialect Geography*, 35–40, 93–94.

[30] H. L. Ginsberg, "The Northwest Semitic Languages," in *Patriarchs* (World History of the Jewish People; B. Mazar, ed; New Brunswick: Rutgers University Press, 1970) 102–6.

The evidence of all these sources—Moabite, Ammonite, Deir ꜥAlla, Aramaic, Phoenician, Ugaritic, and Amarna—will be used to delineate elements of IH. I repeat what I stated above: when regular features of these languages appear in the Bible in limited numbers, we will be justified in flagging these features as IH elements. If we possessed a full complement of data to work with, we would be able to draw numerous isoglosses on the map uniting the non-Hebrew speaking areas to the north and east with the regions of Galilee, Samaria, and Gilead.

In a sense this has been strikingly confirmed by the discovery of the Deir ꜥAlla material. The site is within the borders of biblical Israel, though the language of the texts is not BH of the Judahite variety. B. Halpern has realized the importance of this discovery for our present concern (DAPT = Deir ꜥAlla plaster texts):

> . . . DAPT have altered the face of Hebrew language history. They remind us not to make of Judahite Hebrew a monolith, an unproved norm for the north and east. They caution us to sensitivity to geography—dare one add, to topography and sociology as well—in assessing provisionally the dialectology of Canaan. To my mind, the inscriptions establish that Canaan was linguistically cantonized even in the latest Israelite periods.[31]

I am in complete agreement with Halpern's position, but I believe we can go further. In the present monograph I will apply this finding to the Bible itself. That is to say, I believe we now possess sufficient data with which to work to begin talking about regional varieties of Hebrew even within our biblical corpus. In a forthcoming article, I have collected numerous examples of IH morphological features, based on the methodology outlined above.[32]

Israelian Texts

How then do we identify Israelian compositions? We begin with the assumption that those stories which concern the northern judges and the northern kings originated in the northern regions of the country. It is true that all of biblical literature has reached us through

---

[31]   B. Halpern, "Dialect Distribution in Canaan and the Deir Alla Inscriptions," in *"Working With No Data": Semitic and Egyptian Studies Presented to Thomas O. Lambdin* (ed. D. M. Golomb; Winona Lake, IN: Eisenbrauns, 1987) 119–39, in particular p. 139.

[32]   Rendsburg, "Morphological Evidence."

the filter of Judahite scribal activity, but this does not negate the fact that the aforementioned stories were originally written in northern Israel. An examination of the language of these pericopes reveals that these stories include a disproportionate number of grammatical and lexical items which are non-standard within BH but which often have parallels in Phoenician, Moabite, Aramaic, etc. This is by no means a new discovery; the point was demonstrated long ago by C. F. Burney in his two outstanding commentaries.[33] In the specific case of Kings, Burney's position recently has received confirmation from the work of M. Cogan and H. Tadmor.[34]

It was exactly this approach which led me to identify the poem in 2 Sam 23:1–7 as a northern composition.[35] These seven verses contain no less than six grammatical features which are unusual in BH, but which are paralleled in Aramaic, Phoenician, Ugaritic, and Deir ʿAlla. In addition, two other features were identified as northern traits on internal evidence.

Scholars in the past have found that other biblical books contain large numbers of forms with cognate usages in the languages used to the north and east of Israel. For many years it was recognized that the language of Qoheleth was in many ways unusual, but it was the efforts of M. Dahood which first directed scholarly attention to the proper explanation. Dahood pointed out that there were many similarities between Qoheleth's language and Phoenician.[36] There can be no question that Dahood was on the right track, though in certain ways he overstated his case. In particular, he worded his theory in such a way as to turn Qoheleth into a Phoenician, and for this he was criticized by R. Gordis.[37] However, the evidence cannot be dismissed. A renewed effort to study the problem has now been made by J. R.

---

[33] C. F. Burney, *Notes on the Hebrew Text of the Books of Kings* (Oxford: Clarendon Press, 1903) 208–9; and C. F. Burney, *The Book of Judges* (London: Rivingtons, 1918) 171–76. These two books have been reprinted in one volume with a prolegomenon by W. F. Albright (New York: Ktav, 1970).

[34] M. Cogan and H. Tadmor, *II Kings* (AB 11; Garden City, NY: Doubleday, 1988) 9.

[35] G. A. Rendsburg, "The Northern Origin of 'The Last Words of David' (2 Sam 23,1–7)," *Biblica* 69 (1988) 113–21; and G. A. Rendsburg, "Additional Notes on 'The Last Words of David' (2 Sam 23,1–7)," *Biblica* 70 (1989) 403–8.

[36] M. Dahood, "Canaanite-Phoenician Influence in Qoheleth," *Biblica* 33 (1952) 30–52, 191–221; M. Dahood, "The Language of Qoheleth," *CBQ* 14 (1952) 227–32; and M. Dahood "The Phoenician Background of Qoheleth," *Biblica* 47 (1966) 264–82.

[37] R. Gordis, "Was Koheleth a Phoenician?" *JBL* 74 (1955) 103–14. Note the title of Gordis' article.

Davila. His conclusion is in line with my own opinion, that "the Hebrew of Qoheleth was influenced by a northern dialect of Hebrew."[38]

Another book whose northern character has been suspected on the basis of numerous Phoenician parallels is Proverbs. W. F. Albright wrote an important article on the subject thirty years ago,[39] and more recently H. L. Ginsberg briefly discussed the matter.[40] Among the collections at the end of the book of Proverbs are the sections ascribed to Massaite origin. The Aramaizing character of these verses has been noted by previous scholars. But only recently has Kaufman accurately described this peculiar brand of Hebrew: "It could simply have been written in a Trans-Jordanian pre-exilic dialect to start with!"[41] Consequently, there is probably very little Judahite material in Proverbs, the mentioning of Solomon and Hezekiah (Prov 1:1, 10:1, 25:1) notwithstanding.

The third major representative of biblical wisdom literature, namely the book of Job, is also to be counted as an Israelian composition. While I do not accept all of his specific conclusions, I may cite D. N. Freedman's opinion based on his detailed study of the orthographic practices in Job that "the provenance of the book is northern and its date early."[42] Scholars have always recognized the high degree of Aramaizing in Job. There are now several options by which to proceed. The book may be northern in origin, and thus the IH dialect in which Job is written shares many features with Aramaic. Or, as Kaufman has now proposed, style-switching may be operative, with the author purposefully having portrayed his characters as Transjor-

---

[38] J. R. Davila, "Qoheleth and Northern Hebrew," in *Sopher Mahir: Northwest Semitic Studies Presented to Stanislav Segert* = *Maarav* 5–6 (1990) 69–87, in particular p. 87.

[39] W. F. Albright, "Some Canaanite-Phoenician Sources of Hebrew Wisdom," in *Wisdom in Israel and in the Ancient Near East* (eds. M. Noth and D. W. Thomas; SVT 3; Leiden: E. J. Brill, 1960) 1–15.

[40] Ginsberg, *Israelian Heritage*, 36. See also Y. Avishur, *Stylistic Studies of Word-Pairs in Biblical and Ancient Semitic Literatures* (AOAT 210; Neukirchen-Vluyn: Neukirchener Verlag, 1984) 440 and n. 6, who based his conclusion on Ugaritic parallels more than on Phoenician ones. Both Ginsberg and Avishur have emphasized only Proverbs 1–9, though Albright's study (see preceding note) and my own study of Proverbs suggests that IH influence may be seen throughout the book.

[41] Kaufman, "Classification," 54–55.

[42] D. N. Freedman, "Orthographic Peculiarities in the Book of Job," *Eretz-Israel* 9 (W. F. Albright Volume) (1969) 35–44, in particular p. 43.

danians.[43] I prefer to believe that both analyses are correct, and of course they are not mutually exclusive. That is to say, the book of Job stems from northern Israel, but the author also included an extremely heavy overlay of Transjordanian speech to portray his characters as hailing from Uz and environs.

Another section of the Bible which is in many ways quite similar to Job is the story of Balaam. Here too we meet up with a high Aramaizing tendency, and here too we are dealing with a Transjordanian character.[44] The same conclusions which derive from an analysis of the language of Job also hold for the story of Balaam.[45]

Song of Songs is another book whose northern affinities have long been noticed. A full scale study of the language of this poem remains a desideratum, so for the present I must rely on the brief but very important discussion by S. R. Driver.[46] This position has also been argued effectively by Y. Avishur on the basis of a large number of Ugaritic parallels.[47]

Another obvious source for IH is the book of Hosea, on which C. Rabin has written an excellent article.[48] The various tribal blessings which appear in Genesis 49 and Deuteronomy 33, excluding those of Judah, Simeon, and Benjamin, may also be assumed to be of northern provenance. S. Gevirtz pointed out several IH features in the former collection.[49]

Scholars have also argued for northern origins of selected biblical texts on other, non-linguistic grounds. In two specific cases, I would like to echo these views because I believe the linguistic evidence is

---

[43] Kaufman, "Classification," 55.

[44] See Kaufman, "Classification," 54.

[45] This merits a full investigation. The best study in recent years is S. Morag, "Rovde Qadmut: ʿIyyunim Leshoniyim be-Mishle Bilʿam," *Tarbiz* 50 (1980–81) 1–24. See also my brief comments in Rendsburg, "Northern Origin," 115–16.

[46] Driver, *Introduction*, 448–449. This opinion is cited approvingly by S. Morag, "On the Historical Validity of the Vocalization of the Hebrew Bible," *JAOS* 94 (1974) 308; and with some qualification by A. Hurvitz, "Ha-Lashon ha-ʿIvrit ba-Tequfa ha-Parsit," in *Shivat Ṣiyyon—Yeme Shilton Paras* (Ha-Historiya shel ʿAm Yisraʾel; Jerusalem: Alexander Peli, 1983) 217–18. See also the discussion in M. H. Pope, *Song of Songs* (AB 7C; Garden City, NY: Doubleday, 1977) 33–34, 362.

[47] Y. Avishur, "Le-Ziqa ha-Signonit Beyn Shir ha-Shirim ve-Sifrut ʾUgarit," *Beth Miqra* 59 (1974) 508–25; and Avishur, *Stylistic Studies of Word-Pairs*, 440.

[48] C. Rabin, "Leshonam shel ʿAmos ve-Hosheaʿ," in *ʿIyyunim be-Sefer Tre-ʿAsar* (ed. B. Z. Luria; Jerusalem: Kiryath Sepher, 1981) 117–36.

[49] S. Gevirtz, "Asher in the Blessing of Jacob (Genesis xlix 20)," *VT* 37 (1987) 159–60.

sufficient to bear these positions out.[50] More than a half-century ago, A. C. Welch claimed that Nehemiah 9 originated in the northern kingdom.[51] At first glance, this is a most unlikely claim, but in fact this chapter includes several IH features. A better known attempt to ascribe northern origins to an individual chapter is O. Eissfeldt's contention that Deuteronomy 32 "in einem der mittelpalästinischen Stämme entstanden denken müssen."[52] Here too there is enough linguistic evidence to substantiate the claim.[53]

Before concluding this survey of the sources of IH, two unique sources must be mentioned. The first of these is exilic and post-exilic literature wherein one often encounters northern grammatical features. C. H. Gordon proposed some time ago that this phenomenon is due to the reunion of northern exiles and Judean exiles in Mesopotamia in the 6th Century B.C.E.[54] Moreover, stories such as those in 2 Chronicles 30 and Jer 41:4–5 imply that Israelians continued to dwell in their homeland after 721 B.C.E. and even were loyal to

---

[50] I do not, however, believe that the so-called "E" source and the book of Deuteronomy are northern in origin. The former was attributed to northern Israel by O. Procksch, *Das nordhebräische Sagenbuch, Die Elohimquelle* (Leipzig: J. C. Hinrichs, 1906). For effective counter arguments see O. Eissfeldt, *The Old Testament: An Introduction* (New York: Harper and Row, 1965) 203–204. Many scholars have concluded that Deuteronomy is northern; see most recently Ginsberg, *Israelian Heritage*. But N. Lohfink ("Deuteronomy," in *Interpreter's Dictionary of the Bible. Supplementary Volume* [ed. K. Crim; Nashville: Abingdon, 1976] 229) correctly stated that "judging by the language, the origin of Deuteronomy was more likely in Jerusalem than in the country." My own research has shown that in neither case, not in "E" nor in Deuteronomy, is there a concentration of IH forms; see Rendsburg, "Morphological Evidence."

[51] A. C. Welch, "The Source of Nehemiah IX," *ZAW* 47 (1929) 130–37.

[52] O. Eissfeldt, *Das Lied Moses Deuteronomium 32.1–43 und das Lehrgedicht Asaphs Psalm 78 samt einer Analyse der Umgebung des Mose-Liedes* (Berichte über die Verhandlungen der Sächsischen Akademie der Wissenschaften zu Leipzig, Philologisch-historische Klasse, Band 104, Heft 5) (Berlin: Akademie-Verlag, 1958) 42.

[53] A northern provenance for Deuteronomy 32 has also been posited by E. Nielsen, "Historical Perspectives and Geographical Horizons: On the Question of North-Israelite Elements in Deuteronomy," *ASTI* 11 (1977–78) 82. This is not the case with S. Hidal ("Some Reflections on Deuteronomy 32," *ASTI* 11 [1977–78] 15–21), though he has noted some affinities between Deuteronomy 32 and Nehemiah 9 (p. 19). Since the latter is most probably a northern composition (see above), this point strengthens the argument for an Israelian origin of the former.

[54] C. H. Gordon, "North Israelite Influence on Postexilic Hebrew," *IEJ* 5 (1955) 85–88. This view has been accepted by Kutscher, *A History of the Hebrew Language*, 55.

Jerusalem.[55] Through such minglings of northerners and southerners in the 7th, 6th, and 5th Centuries B.C.E., one understands how exilic and post-exilic books sometimes admit northern grammatical features. Accordingly, in the discussion below, I will occasionally refer to such books.

The final source of IH to be noted in this survey is the language of the prophetic speeches directed to the foreign nations. It is my contention that these addresses very often are couched in the dialects of the addressee nations. Some work on the rhetoric of the prophets in this regard has already been done.[56] I would merely extend the discussion to include linguistic evidence as well.

Psalms Research

Above I noted that in the past scholars have argued for a northern provenance for selected psalms. Although only rarely have these hypotheses considered the linguistic evidence, they merit our attention nonetheless. The most celebrated case of a proposed northern composition is Psalm 29. H. Gunkel had already suggested that this poem emanated from the north on the basis of the references to Lebanon and Sirion in vv. 5–6.[57] This opinion was given strong support by Ginsberg's analysis in the wake of the discovery of the Ugaritic texts,[58] and virtually all treatments since the 1930's have concurred with this view.[59]

---

[55] See S. Japhet, "People and Land in the Restoration Period," in *Das Land Israel in biblischer Zeit* (ed. G. Strecker; Göttingen: Vandenhoeck & Ruprecht, 1983) 105.

[56] See most importantly P. Machinist, "Assyria and Its Image in the First Isaiah," *JAOS* 103 (1983) 719–37.

[57] H. Gunkel, *Die Psalmen* (HKAT; Göttingen: Vandenhoeck & Ruprecht, 1926) 125.

[58] H. L. Ginsberg, "A Phoenician Hymn in the Psalter," in *Atti del XIX Congresso Internazionale degli Orientalisti (Roma 1935)* (Rome: G. Bardi, 1938) 472–76; and H. L. Ginsberg, *Kitve ʾUgarit* (Jerusalem: Bialik, 1936) 129–31. More recently see H. L. Ginsberg, "A Strand in the Cord of Hebraic Hymnody," *Eretz-Israel* 9 (W. F. Albright Volume) (1969) 45 n. 2.

[59] See, e.g., T. H. Gaster, "Psalm 29," *JQR* 37 (1946–47) 55–65; F. M. Cross, "Notes on a Canaanite Psalm in the Old Testament," *BASOR* 117 (1950) 19–21; F. M. Cross, *Canaanite Myth and Hebrew Epic* (Cambridge, MA: Harvard University Press, 1973) 151–56; O. Loretz, *Psalm 29: Kanaanäische El- und Baaltraditionen in jüdischer Sicht* (UBL 2; Soest: CIS-Verlag, 1984); C. Kloos, *YHWH's Combat with the Sea* (Leiden: E. J. Brill, 1986) 13–124; Avishur, *Stylistic Studies of Word-Pairs*, 440, and his reference in n. 3. Only B. Margulis, "The Canaanite Origin of Psalm 29

The Korah and Asaph poems, both as collections and as individual psalms, have been the focus of much discussion in this regard. M. J. Buss wrote a short article in which he concluded that "a number of the Asaphite psalms contain indications that they are of North-Israelite origin, or that they have at least an interest in the affairs of the northern kingdom."[60] H. P. Nasuti recently devoted an entire monograph to the Asaph psalms.[61] Although he never makes the explicit claim that they are northern in origin, he does place them within the "Ephraimite tradition stream," a term which he borrows from his mentor R. R. Wilson.[62]

The first attempt to ascribe the Korah psalms to northern Israel was that of J. Peters.[63] More specifically, he believed that the collection represented the liturgy for the festival of Sukkot as celebrated in the shrine at Dan. Lately, M. D. Goider published a monograph essentially agreeing with Peters' position.[64]

Other scholars have suggested a northern provenance for individual Asaph or Korah psalms. They include Gunkel on Psalms 45, 77, 80, 81[65]; J. Morgenstern on Psalms 48 and 82[66]; Eissfeldt on Psalm 80[67]; S. Loewenstamm on Psalm 81[68]; Ginsberg on Psalms 47, 77, 80, and 81[69]; and at least tentatively R. P. Carroll on Psalm 78.[70] In all

---

Reconsidered," *Biblica* 51 (1970) 332–48, has been a major voice opposed to the northern origin of Psalm 29, but few have been convinced by his position.

[60] M. J. Buss, "The Psalms of Asaph and Korah," *JBL* 82 (1963) 382–92, in particular p. 384.

[61] H. P. Nasuti, *Tradition History and the Psalms of Asaph* (SBLDS 88; Atlanta: Scholars Press, 1988).

[62] R. R. Wilson, *Prophecy and Society in Ancient Israel* (Philadelphia: Fortress, 1980) 17–18.

[63] J. Peters, *The Psalms as Liturgies* (New York: Macmillan, 1922). See also J. Peters, "A Jerusalem Processional," *JPOS* 1 (1920), pp. 36–41.

[64] M. D. Goulder, *The Psalms of the Sons of Korah* (JSOTSS 20; Sheffield: JSOT Press, 1982).

[65] Gunkel, *Psalmen*, 193, 335, 353, 359.

[66] J. Morgenstern, "Psalm 48," *HUCA* 16 (1941) 93; and J. Morgenstern, "The Mythological Background of Psalm 82," *HUCA* 14 (1939) 80–81 n. 88, 121–24.

[67] O. Eissfeldt, "Psalm 80," in *Geschichte und Altes Testament: Albrecht Alt zum 70. Geburtstag dargebracht* (Tübingen: J. C. B. Mohr, 1953) 65–78 (reprinted in O. Eissfeldt, *Kleine Schriften* [6 vols; Tübingen: J. C. B. Mohr, 1962–79] 3.221–32); and O. Eissfeldt, "Psalm 80 und Psalm 89," *WO* 3 (1964–66) 27–31 (reprinted in Eissfeldt, *Kleine Schriften*, 4.132–36).

[68] S. Loewenstamm, "ʿēdût bîhôsēp," *Eretz-Israel* 5 (Benjamin Mazar Volume) (1958) 80–82.

[69] Ginsberg, *Israelian Heritage*, 31–34.

these cases, the claim for northern origin has been based almost wholly on historical and literary considerations, with linguistic evidence hardly ever entering into the discussion.

Methodology

In the analysis which follows I will confirm the northern provenance of the individual poems just mentioned as well as that of selected other chapters. How can one be sure that the linguistic material I will present in actuality points to northern composition? My approach is to adapt the procedures introduced by Hurvitz for the study of LBH to the study of IH.[71] In Hurvitz's work, he has emphasized four factors: distribution, extra-biblical sources, opposition, and concentration. A brief explanation of these terms as applied to the study of IH now follows.

"Distribution" refers to where in the Bible a particular feature appears. If a suspected IH element is limited to texts such as the stories of the northern judges and northern kings, the Balaam oracles, the book of Job, etc., I will assume that it is characteristic of a northern dialect. Even if an occasional example of a suspected IH feature appears in a patently JH text, this still will be considered sufficient distribution to qualify as an IH feature. For example, if a presumed IH element occurs 15 times in northern texts and 3 times in Judahite works, this will not disqualify its inclusion as a piece of evidence in favor of the northern origin of a particular psalm. Since the ratio of Judahite literature to Israelian literature within the entire corpus of the Bible is considerable (I estimate 4:1), an example such as the above becomes even more strikingly northern in distribution.[72] Moreover, as we know is the case in contemporary English, learned writers often borrow words from a dialect other than their own. For example, while Americans generally do not use the words "flat" (= apartment), "lorry" (= truck), "lift" (= elevator), etc., one does encounter these Britishisms in American English occasionally.

"Extra-biblical sources" refers to the Northwest Semitic material discussed above. As already mentioned, a catalyst for recognizing a

---

[70] R. P. Carroll, "Psalm lxxviii: Vestiges of a Tribal Polemic," *VT* 21 (1971) 134 n. 2, 144.

[71] For the most succinct statement see Hurvitz, "Ha-Lashon ha-ʿIvrit ba-Tequfa ha-Parsit," 222–23. For extended discussion see Hurvitz, *Beyn Lashon le-Lashon*, 67–69.

[72] Here I follow the methodology outlined by Tsevat, *A Study of the Language of the Biblical Psalms*, 7–8.

particular grammatical element as northern will be its presence in Aramaic, Phoenician, etc.

"Opposition" refers to a distinction which can be posited between IH and JH. If a particular feature appears only in IH texts, it is possible that it is only coincidental that it is absent in JH works. This is especially true if the lexeme or morpheme or syntagma under discussion is a *hapax legomenon* or a *dislegomenon*. Accordingly, often it will be necessary to demonstrate that IH utilizes a particular element in contrast to the corresponding JH feature.

I will admit from the outset that I will not be able to satisfy these three criteria in all cases. However, in such instances, it is always due to lack of evidence, and not to contradictory evidence. Nonetheless, caution is advisable. If at times it appears that words such as "probably" and "most likely" are being used too frequently, it is only because of our inability to see the total picture. My assumption is, were we to be blessed with a complete view of the geographical dialects of ancient Israel, we would be able to rid ourselves of such qualifications.

Once these three criteria have been met to sufficient satisfaction, it will be possible to categorize a particular usage as an IH characteristic. It will then become apparent, as mentioned earlier, that a "concentration" of such usages occurs in selected psalms. This will be the test which a poem itself must pass before it qualifies as northern in origin. In other words, if only one or two IH elements appear(s) in an individual chapter, this will be deemed insufficient evidence for postulating northern provenance.[73] In the individual psalms to be treated in our study, there is always a significant bunching of IH features.

The Masoretic Text

One additional issue needs to be raised before proceeding with our investigation. That issue is the trustworthiness of MT, not only its consonantal text but its vocalization as well. Here I wish to echo once more Hurvitz's opinion. He correctly stated that "a linguistic study whose central purpose is to seek facts and avoid conjectures, should base itself on *actual* texts—difficult though they may be—rather than depend on *reconstructed* texts."[74] As far as the vocalization is con-

---

[73] The only exceptions to this will be the general discussions of the Korah and Asaph collections. See below, Chapters VI and X.

[74] Hurvitz, *Priestly Source and the Book of Ezekiel*, 19.

cerned, here I would direct the reader to the writings of J. Barr and S. Morag,[75] whose opinions I accept wholeheartedly.

The only exceptions to this dictum are instances where the Masora no longer recognized ancient forms. Examples include Ps 16:2, where it seems clear that *ʾāmart* means "I say" (not "you [fsg] say"), and Ps 50:10, where the conjunction *p* should be restored. But passages such as these are rare. Generally, I will work with MT and often in the notes I will point out the unnecessity of textual emendation.

It should also be noted that it is improper to speak of MT as if it constituted but one textual witness. As H. M. Orlinsky has emphasized in his research, our received text is the conflation of different texts, with variants noted in the Kethiv-Qere system.[76] Theoretically these differences within MT are all valid textual witnesses. Accordingly, in my investigation into northern linguistic elements in biblical texts, I will at times cite Kethiv forms and at other times cite Qere forms.

With the foregoing as introduction, we may now proceed to an investigation of the individual psalms in which IH features cluster.[77]

---

[75] J. Barr, *Comparative Philology and the Text of the Old Testament* (Oxford: Clarendon, 1968) 221; and Morag, "On the Historical Validity of the Vocalization of the Hebrew Bible," 307–15.

[76] H. M. Orlinsky, "The Origins of the Kethib-Qere System: A New Approach," *Congress Volume Oxford 1959* (SVT 7; Leiden: E. J. Brill, 1960) 184–92; and H. M. Orlinsky, "Prolegomenon" to C. D. Ginsburg, *Introduction to the Massoretico-Critical Edition of the Hebrew Bible* (New York: Ktav, 1966) I–XLV.

[77] In the discussions which follow, points are cited according to the following system: Roman numerals stand for chapters within this book, Arabic numerals stand for points raised within a particular chapter. Thus, for example, II.4 stands for Chapter II, point 4.

Chapter I

Psalms 9–10

1. In Ps 9:7 the word ʿārîm appears parallel to the word ʾôyēb "enemy."[1] It is patent that the usual meaning of ʿārîm, namely "cities," does not fit the context in this verse. Instead, we should assume the meaning "adversaries," with ʿārîm understood as the IH equivalent to standard Hebrew ṣārîm. The proto-Semitic root of this word is ḍrr, as demonstrated by the appearance of this root in Arabic, Old South Arabic, and Ethiopic with the meaning "fight, injure, hostile." The normal reflex of this root in Hebrew is ṣrr[2]; in Aramaic it appears as ʿrr.[3] For our interpretation of Ps 9:7 to be correct, we will have to assume that in some areas of northern Israel the reflex of proto-Semitic ḍ was also ʿ. As Rabin has shown, IH phonology shares certain isoglosses with Aramaic, and not with JH.[4]

This understanding of ʿārîm in Ps 9:7 is bolstered by several other points. First, as R. Gordis pointed out, "the verb ntš is never used of cities, only of living things, generally of human beings" (see 1 Kgs 14:15, Jer 12:14, 12:17, 2 Chr 7:20).[5] Secondly, the lexeme ʿār- "adversary" occurs elsewhere in the Bible in 1 Sam 28:16, Ps 139:20

---

[1] For an extended discussion see G. Schmuttermayr, *Psalm 9–10: Studien zur Textkritik und Übersetzung* (St. Ottilien: EOS Verlag, 1985) 54–62.

[2] BDB, 865; and KB, 818.

[3] BDB, 1108; KB, 1111; M. Jastrow, *A Dictionary of the Targumim, the Talmud Babli and Yerushalmi, and the Midrashic Literature* (2 vols; London: Luzac, 1903) 2.1123–24; and W. H. Rossell, *A Handbook of Aramaic Magical Texts* (Ringwood Borough, NJ: Shelton College, 1955) 144.

[4] C. Rabin, "The Emergence of Classical Hebrew," in *The Age of the Monarchies: Culture and Society* (World History of the Jewish People; ed. A. Malamat; Jerusalem: Massada Press, 1979) 293 n. 4; and Rabin, "ʿAmos ve-Hosheaʿ," 120.

[5] R. Gordis, "Psalm 9–10—A Textual and Exegetical Study," *JQR* 48 (1958) 111.

(see also Dan 4:16 for the Aramaic form).[6] In the first of these passages, the context places us in northern Israel. The speaker is Samuel of Ephraim and the setting is Endor in Manasseh. In the second of these passages, I would not argue for any northern connection; instead the psalm is probably a post-exilic composition as evidenced by the large number of Aramaisms it contains. Furthermore, it should be noted that the pairing of *ʾōyēb* and *ʿārîm* is consistent with the collocation of the roots *ʾyb* and *ṣrr* in Northwest Semitic texts such as Exod 23:22, Deut 32:27, Ps 13:5, etc., and *UT* 68:8–9, ʿnt:III:34, ʿnt:IV:48–50.[7] Finally, our interpretation of Ps 9:7 clears up two other difficulties in the verse. The pronominal suffix on *zikrām* "their memory" is masculine plural, which accords with *ʿārîm* = "adversaries," but not with *ʿārîm* = "cities," which is feminine.[8] Secondly, we probably can now explain the enigmatic *hēmmāh* at the end of the verse.[9] Here I would appeal to the proposal of A. D. Corre to understand *hēmmāh* in other biblical passages as equivalent to English/Latin *sic*.[10] In the present instance the scribe wished to call attention to the fact that indeed he had copied the words correctly and that *ʿrym* was not an error for *ṣrym*. Accordingly, Ps 9:7b is to be translated "You have uprooted the adversaries, their memory is perished (*sic*)."

2.   Twice in this poem the relative pronoun *zû* appears, in Ps 9:16 *běrešet zû ṭāmānû* "in the net in which they hid" and Ps 10:2 *bimmězimmôt zû ḥāšābû* "in the schemes which they devised." Admittedly, the relative pronoun *zû* is not limited to IH. The form is an archaic one which was utilized throughout ancient Israel as a poetic variant to prose particles such as *ʾăšer* and *še-* (Exod 15:13, 15:16, 68:29, etc.).[11] Yet the following factors should be taken into consider-

---

[6]   See S. R. Driver, *Notes on the Hebrew Text of the Books of Samuel* (Oxford: Clarendon, 1890) 167–68.

[7]   M. Dahood, "Ugaritic-Hebrew Parallel Pairs," in *Ras Shamra Parallels* (3 vols.; eds. L. R. Fisher [and S. Rummel]; AnOr 49–51; Rome: Pontifical Biblical Institute, 1972–81) 1.97–98; and Avishur, *Stylistic Studies of Word-Pairs*, 344–46.

[8]   I do not mean to imply that gender discord cannot occur in BH, for there are dozens of such instances in the Bible. See Rendsburg, *Diglossia in Ancient Hebrew*, ch. 2; R. J. Ratner, *Gender Problems in Biblical Hebrew* (Ph.D. dissertation, Hebrew Union College-Jewish Institute of Religion, Cincinnati 1983) 26–56; and J. Levi, *Die Inkongruenz im biblischen Hebräisch* (Wiesbaden: Otto Harrassowitz, 1987). Still, one expects gender agreement and we have restored the norm with our explication of Ps 9:7.

[9]   For discussion see Schmuttermayr, *Psalm 9–10*, 62–76.

[10]   A. D. Corre, "*ʾēlle, hēmma = sic*," *Biblica* 54 (1973) 263–64.

[11]   Robertson, *Linguistic Evidence*, 62–65.

ation: 1) its cognates in Northwest Semitic are Byblian *z*, Aramaic and Samalian *zy*;[12] and 2) its partner *zeh* occurs in Judg 5:5 which is clearly northern, Prov 23:22 where northern provenance is probable,[13] and Job 15:17, 19:19 where we are again dealing with an Israelian dialect (see above, p. 10). Therefore I would claim the following: the relative pronoun *zû/zeh* is not solely characteristic of IH, i.e., its presence in a poem is not sufficient grounds to claim northern origin, yet when other indications of northern composition are present the use of *zû/zeh* may be incorporated into the total picture as part of the cumulative evidence. Presumably this is even more the case when *zû* is attested twice in a single poem.

3. Ps 10:1 begins as follows: *lāmāh yhwh taʿămōd bĕrāḥôq* "why O Yahweh do you stand from afar?" The preposition which usually governs the verb *ʿmd* in such contexts is *m(n)* "from" (see Exod 20:18, 20:21, 1 Sam 26:13, 2 Kgs 2:7, Isa 59:14, Ps 38:12),[14] but in the present instance it is *b*. In the past scholars have been apt to emend Ps 10:1 to read *mērāḥôq*.[15] However, this is clearly a case of the interchange of the prepositions *b*, *l*, and *m(n)* now well attested in the Bible, so that no emendation is necessary.[16]

Many scholars are of the opinion that this interchange is a standard feature of the entire biblical corpus,[17] but Z. Zevit has raised some serious objections to this view.[18] Moreover, his call for a complete detailed study of the subject has never been answered.[19] I also

---

[12] Garr, *Dialect Geography*, 85.

[13] See Rendsburg, "Northern Origin," 117.

[14] N. M. Sarna, "The Interchange of the Prepositions *Beth* and *Min* in Biblical Hebrew," *JBL* 78 (1959) 312.

[15] See, e.g., C. A. Briggs, *A Critical and Exegetical Commentary on the Book of Psalms*, 2 vols. (ICC; New York: Charles Scribner's Sons, 1906–7) 1.85.

[16] J. Reider, "Miscellanea Hebraica," *JJS* 3 (1952) 78; Gordis, "Psalm 9–10," 111–12; and M. Dahood, *Psalms I* (AB 16; Garden City, NY: Doubleday, 1966) 61. For a detailed treatment see Schmuttermayr, *Psalm 9–10*, 101–13.

[17] Sarna, "Interchange"; M. Dahood, *Psalms III* (AB 17A; Garden City, NY: Doubleday, 1970) 391–95; A. C. M. Blommerde, *Northwest Semitic Grammar and Job* (Rome: Pontifical Biblical Institute, 1969) 19–21; and G. Schmuttermayr, "Ambivalenz und Aspektdifferenz: Bemerkungen zu den hebräischen Präpositionen *b*, *l*, und *mn*," *BZ* 15 (1971) 29–51.

[18] Z. Zevit, "The So-Called Interchangeability of the Prepositions *b*, *l*, and *m(n)* in Northwest Semitic," *JANES* 7 (1975) 103–11.

[19] Ibid., 111: "What is desired is an inner Hebrew study. . . . All verbs which are coordinated with at least two proclitic prepositions should be isolated and their semantic and syntactic contexts described, catalogued, and compared. . . .

have no intentions of conducting such an investigation here, but I would like to underscore one of Zevit's points and posit a working hypothesis. Zevit noted that in Phoenician not until the 4th Century B.C.E. do we have the first appearance of ablative *m(n)*, suggesting that *b* and *l* served to express "from" in this language prior to this time.[20]

Biblical evidence suggests that the same situation holds for IH. Again, I cannot claim to have conducted an exhaustive search, but it is apparent that a good number of the biblical instances of *b/l* = "from" appear in northern contexts. Note the following five examples:

Josh 3:16K	*harḥēq mēʾōd bēʾādām* (Q: *mēʾādām*)
	"very far from Adam"
2 Kgs 4:24	*ʾal taʿăṣor lî lirkōb*
	"do not prevent me from riding"
2 Kgs 14:13	*bēšaʿar ʾeprayim ʿad šaʿar happināh*
	"from the gate of Ephraim unto the corner gate"
2 Kgs 14:28	*hēšib ʾet dammeśeq wēʾet ḥămāt lîhûdāh bēyiśrāʾēl*
	"he retrieved Damascus and Hamath from Yehuda (= Samʾal) for Israel"[21]
Ps 29:10	*yhwh lammabbûl yāšāb*
	"Yahweh has reigned from (= since) the flood"
Ps 140:11	*bēmahămōrôt bal yāqûmû*
	"from the deep pits they will not arise"

Once collected, the data should be analyzed with an eye to the synchronic and diachronic distribution of the phenomena insofar as this is possible."

[20] As Zevit ("Interchangeability," 109) noted, the situation in Phoenician is similar to Ugaritic. The Ugaritic poetic texts, presumably composed in a more archaic idiom, employ only *b* and *l*. But the prose texts, where innovative usages are more likely to appear, include the one attestation of *m*. See M. Liverani, "Elementi innovativi nell'Ugaritico non letterario," *Atti della Accademia nazionale dei Lincei, Rendiconti della Classe di scienze morali, storiche e filologiche*, Series VIII, Vol. 19, No. 5–6 (1964) 173–91, especially p. 188. Should this be used as another point to bolster the classification system of Ginsberg ("The Northwest Semitic Languages," 102–124), with a Phoenic group consisting of Phoenician and Ugaritic distinguished from a Hebraic group consisting of Hebrew and Moabite? I am content merely to raise the issue without entering into further discussion.

[21] For the proper understanding of this verse, see C. H. Gordon, *Ugaritic Textbook* (Rome: Pontifical Biblical Institute, 1967) 92; and C. H. Gordon, *The Ancient Near East* (New York: Norton, 1965) 219.

These passages all have northern settings. The first concerns a city in the territory of Manasseh; the second appears in a story of the northern prophet Elisha; the third and fourth occur in the records of Israelian kings (Jehoash and Jeroboam II, respectively); the fifth occurs in a poem which refers to northern locales such as Lebanon, Sirion, and Kadesh, and mentions northern flora such as cedars and forests (see below III.1); and the last occurs in a poem with numerous features of IH (see below XIV.6).

In light of this evidence, I am inclined to consider the ablative use of *b/l* a feature of IH.[22] I repeat that this proposal is but a working hypothesis, and I agree that it merits further study along the lines called for by Zevit, but for the nonce I believe the conclusion is defensible. Accordingly, the usage *rḥq b-* instead of *rḥq m(n)* in Ps 10:1 is another indicator of this psalm's northern origin.

4. Most scholars agree that *gaʾăwat* "haughtiness" cannot be the *nomen regens* for the following word *rāšāʿ* "wicked" in Ps 10:2.[23] Two solutions generally have been proposed: 1) to add a pronominal suffix with the resultant reading *gaʾăwātô*[24]; and 2) to revocalize the form to *gēʾût*.[25] Neither of these options is necessary, however, especially in view of my comments at the outset concerning the received text, consonants and vowels. Instead, the proper solution was proposed by Gordis, simply to understand *gaʾăwat* as a noun in the absolute state with the *-at* preserved.[26] As is well known, this ending *-at* occurs in most of the Canaanite dialects (JH and Deir ʿAlla are two exceptions) as well as in Aramaic in nouns derived from IIIw/y roots.[27]

Many examples of feminine singular nouns ending in *-āt* (in absolute or construct state) and *-at* (in the absolute state) in the Bible are to be explained as northernisms.[28] This is borne out by the following instances of this usage: *šipʿat* "multitude" in 2 Kgs 9:17 appears in a

---

22 Rendsburg, "Morphological Evidence."

23 For discussion see Schmuttermayr, *Psalm 9–10*, 114–16.

24 E.g., J. Leveen, "Psalm X: A Reconstruction," *JTS* 45 (1944) 17.

25 E.g., H.-J. Kraus, *Psalmen* (2 vols.; Neukirchen: Neukirchener Verlag, 1960) 1.76.

26 Gordis, "Psalm 9–10," 112.

27 Garr, *Dialect Geography*, 59–60, 93–94; and S. Segert, *Altaramäische Grammatik* (Leipzig, VEB Verlag, 1975) 206–7.

28 Rendsburg, "Morphological Evidence." Other instances of this usage are simply archaic poetic diction, e.g., *pōrāt* "fruitful" (?) in Gen 49:22 (bis), *zimrāt* "strength/song" in Exod 15:2, Is 12:2, Ps 118:14; or they are Aramaisms, e.g., *qěṣāt* "end" in Dan 1:2, 1:5, 1:15, 1:18, Neh 7:20; or they may even be Akkadianisms, e.g., *bārqat* "emerald" in Ezek 28:13 = Akkadian *barraqtu*.

story about the northern kings Jehoram and Jehu and is actually placed in the mouth of an Israelian scout; Jeremiah utilizes the words *yitrat* "abundance" in Jer 48:36 and *těhillat* "praise" in Jer 49:25Q in speeches aimed at Moab and Damascus, respectively; the forms *měnāt* "portion" in Ps 16:5 and *naḥălāt* "heritage" in Ps 16:6, occur in a psalm with other northern affinities (see below II.3); the musical instruments *maḥălāt* in Ps 53:1, 88:1, and *něgînat* in Ps 61:1 may have been borrowed from Canaanites who preserved the -*at* suffix (on the former term see below VI.14, VII.2); the form *ḥayyat* "beast" in Ps 74:19 occurs in a northern composition (see below IX.8); the form *šěnat* "sleep" in Ps 132:4 occurs in a northern poem (see below XII.2), and *mě'at* "hundred" in Qoh 8:12 is explicable if we agree to the northern origin of Qoheleth.

The evidence from toponyms which retain -*āt*/-*at* is also germane, in that they are concentrated mainly in the north: two in Asher (*ḥelqat, libnāt*), three in Naphtali (*ḥammat, ʿănāt, raqqat*), one in Issachar (*ʾănāḥărāt*), one in Zebulun (*dābrat*), one in Ephraim (*mikmětāt*), and two in Transjordan (*ṭabbāt, qěnāt*).

In light of this evidence, there is no justification to alter in any manner MT at Ps 10:2. The form *gaʾăwat* should be accepted as the IH equivalent for JH *gaʾăwāh*.

5.   The negative particle *bal* occurs five times in Psalm 10, in vv. 4, 6, 11, 15, 18. This is the standard term used in Phoenician[29]—the form *lʾ* in fact appears not at all[30]; and *bl* is common in Ugaritic as well.[31] We have reason, therefore, to suspect that *bal* was an IH trait. This suspicion is borne out by the distribution of *bal* in the Bible.

Elsewhere in Psalms *bal* occurs as follows: four times in Psalm 16 (see below II.1), twice in the Korah collection (see below VI.8), once in Psalm 58 (see below VIII.8), once in the Asaph group (see below X.15), twice in Psalm 140 (see below XIV.7), and once in Psalm 141 (see below XV.3). All of these contain numerous other IH elements which reveal them to be northern compositions. Outside of Psalms

---

[29]   J. Friedrich and W. Röllig, *Phönizisch-punische Grammatik* (2nd ed.; Rome: Pontifical Biblical Institute, 1970) 125; and R. S. Tomback, *A Comparative Semitic Lexicon of the Phoenician and Punic Languages* (SBLDS 32; Missoula, MT: Scholars Press, 1978) 46.

[30]   See Friedrich and Röllig, *Phönizisch-punische Grammatik*, 161; and Ginsberg, "The Northwest Semitic Languages," 109.

[31]   Gordon, *Ugaritic Textbook*, 372; and J. Aistleitner, *Wörterbuch der ugaritischen Sprache* (Berlin: Akademie Verlag, 1963) 49.

bal occurs twice in Hosea, ten times in Proverbs, and once in Job, all of which are Israelian texts.

Now it is true that *bal* occurs in unmistakably Jerusalemite compositions, e.g., numerous times in Isaiah and in other Psalms which lack additional IH features. But as the above survey indicates, the form occurs disproportionately in northern texts. Consequently, the concentration of five instances of *bal* in Psalm 10 is an indication of the northern origin of these verses.

6. In Ps 10:13 we encounter the interrogative pronoun *meh* "what" before the word *niʾēṣ*. According to the norms of Hebrew grammar, *meh* occurs before words beginning with *ʿā, ḥā*, and *hā*.[32] However, it also stands before non-laryngeal consonants not infrequently, namely: Exod 22:26, 33:16, Judg 16:5 (bis), 16:6 (bis), 16:10, 16:13, 16:15, 1 Sam 1:8 (tris), 4:6, 6:2, 15:14, 29:4, 1 Kgs 22:16, 2 Kgs 1:7, 4:13, 4:14, Isa 1:5, 2:22, Jer 8:9, 16:10, Hag 1:9, Mal 1:6, 1:7, 3:7, 3:8, Ps 4:3, 10:13, 119:9, Prov 4:19, 31:2, Job 7:21. (This list includes attestations of *lāmeh, kammeh*, and *bammeh*.)

An investigation of these passages reveals that a disproportionate number occur in non-Judahite contexts. In the seven instances in Judges 16 and in 1 Sam 4:6, 6:2, 29:4 it is the Philistines who are speaking; in 1 Sam 1:8 (tris) it is Elkanah of Ephraim; in 1 Sam 4:14 it is Eli priest of Shiloh; in 1 Sam 15:14 it is Samuel of Ephraim; in 1 Kgs 22:16 it is the Israelian king Ahab; in 2 Kgs 1:7 it is his son Ahaziah; in 2 Kgs 4:13, 4:14 it is the northern prophet Elisha; Prov 4:19 occurs in a section replete with northernisms; in Prov 31:2 we have the words of Lemuel king of Massa; and of course Job 7:21 places us once again outside Judah. If we now include *meh* in Ps 10:13, a total of 23 out of the 36 attestations, or 64%, of *meh* before a non-laryngeal consonant are in non-Judahite contexts. (If we further include the post-exilic examples Hag 1:9, Mal 1:6, 1:7, 3:7, 3:8, for the reasons stated earlier, then 28 out of 36, or 78%, of these usages could be classified as IH.) Given the fact that the vast majority of biblical literature stems from Judah, specifically Jerusalem, statistically these figures are even more striking (see above, p. 15). They indicate that the Masora has preserved for us a feature with an isogloss stretching from Philistia in the southwest[33] through the area of northern Israel to Massa in the

---

[32] H. Bauer and P. Leander, *Historische Grammatik der hebräischen Sprache des Alten Testamentes* (Halle: Max Niemeyer, 1922) 266.

[33] Ginsberg ("The Northwest Semitic Languages," 110–11) has already postulated including Philistine in his Phoenic group.

northeast.[34] This in turn provides additional evidence for establishing the northern provenance of Psalms 9–10.

7.   In Ps 10:14 we read *hāyîtâ ʿôzēr* "you were helping," one of the clearest cases of the periphrastic perfect in the Bible. As is well known, this construction is especially common in Aramaic[35] and in Mishnaic Hebrew.[36] In the Bible it occurs about thirty times.[37] The many examples in Daniel (8:5, 8:7, 10:2, 10:9) and Nehemiah (3:26, 5:18, 6:14, 6:19 [bis]) are clearly the result of Aramaic influence. If we exclude these nine instances, we are left with about twenty cases of this usage, ten of which appear in contexts where northern provenance is probable. 2 Sam 3:6, 3:17 concern Abner of the house of Saul; 1 Kgs 22:35, 2 Kgs 6:8, 17:33 (bis), 17:41, 2 Chr 18:34 all concern the northern kingdom of Israel; and Job 1:14 places us in a non-Judahite setting. This distribution permits us to view this syntagma as a grammatical feature linking Israelian and Aramean territory.[38] Consequently, the presence of the periphrastic perfect in Psalms 9–10 is another point in favor of this poem's northern provenance.

Summary

These seven grammatical points clustered in one psalm are sufficient evidence to posit a northern origin for Psalms 9–10. J. Leveen stated that "Psalm X has perhaps more *cruces* than any other passage of equal length in the Hebrew Bible."[39] The hyperbolic nature of this claim aside, we can now provide an answer as to why Psalm 10 is so difficult. It simply is not written in the standard Judahite dialect which we are more accustomed to reading. It is written in a northern

---

[34] On the location of Massa see I. Eph'al, *The Ancient Arabs* (Jerusalem: Magnes, 1982) 218–19.

[35] See the survey by J. C. Greenfield, "The 'Periphrastic Imperative' in Aramaic and Hebrew," *IEJ* 19 (1'369) 206–7.

[36] M. H. Segal, *A Grammar of Mishnaic Hebrew* (Oxford: Clarendon, 1927) 156; and M. Z. Segal, *Diqduq Leshon ha-Mishna* (Tel-Aviv: Dvir, 1936) 182. On the northern affinities of Mishnaic Hebrew, see G. A. Rendsburg, "The Galilean Background of Mishnaic Hebrew," in *Proceedings of the First International Conference on Galilean Studies in Late Antiquity* (ed. L. Levine; forthcoming).

[37] For documentation see S. R. Driver, *A Treatise on the Use of the Tenses in Hebrew* (Oxford: Clarendon, 1892) 170–71; G. Bergsträsser, *Hebräische Grammatik* (Leipzig: F. C. W. Vogel, 1918) 73; and P. Joüon, *Grammaire de l'hébreu biblique* (Rome: Pontifical Biblical Institute, 1923) 340–41.

[38] See further Rabin, "The Emergence of Classical Hebrew," 72.

[39] Leveen, "Psalm X," 16.

dialect which presents many more difficulties for the biblical scholar.[40]

Most scholars have contended that Psalms 9–10 are not two distinct poems, as MT treats them, but rather one continuous composition.[41] Arguments advanced are the apparent alphabetic acrostic which originally may have spanned the two psalms, the lack of a superscription to Psalm 10, and the presence of similar expressions in the two chapters. To this evidence may now be added the fact that northernisms bridge the two chapters, e.g., the use of *zû* as the relative particle in 9:16, 10:2. It is true that the description of Yahweh as *yôšēb ṣiyyôn* "dweller of Zion" in Ps 9:12 and the use of *bat ṣiyyôn* "daughter Zion" in Ps 9:15 may point to a Jerusalemite origin for Psalm 9. But as we shall see below in other instances, a Zion theology does not *a priori* exclude a northern origin. Obviously there were northerners who accepted the official Israelite position concerning the centrality of Zion and Jerusalem. The poet of Psalms 9–10 was one such individual.

---

[40] Among the additional linguistic oddities in the text, I shall note just two, though lack of comparative evidence prevents us from determining whether these elements are also characteristic of IH. The first is the masculine singular imperative *nĕšāʾ* "raise" in Ps 10:12, in place of the expected *šāʾ*. This may represent a geographical variation, but there is no way of establishing this fact given the relative dearth of texts in IH, Phoenician, etc. Similarly, the vocables *ḥēlĕkāh* in 10:8, *ḥēlkāʾîm* in 10:10, and *ḥēlekāh* in 10:14 appear nowhere else in the Bible. Their meaning "humbled, overwhelmed" seems assured, both by the context of Psalm 10 and by the use of the word in Egyptian texts where it appears as a Canaanitism; see W. G. Simpson, "Some Egyptian Light on a Translation Problem in Psalm X," *VT* 19 (1969) 128–31. But we cannot determine whether or not this word was at home in northern Canaan more so than in Jerusalem, so this is a moot point.

[41] Briggs, *Psalms,* 1.68; H. Junker, "Unité, composition et genre littéraire des psaumes IX et X," *RB* 60 (1953) 161–69; Gordis, "Psalm 9–10," 104–8; Kraus, *Psalmen,* 1.77; and Dahood, *Psalms I,* 54.

CHAPTER II

Psalm 16

1. Again there is a marked tendency to use *bal* as the negative particle. It appears four times in this psalm, in vv. 2, 4 (bis), 8. As was the case in Psalms 9–10 (see above I.5), such a concentration is an argument in favor of the northern origin of Psalm 16.

2. The expression *ʾāmart layhwh* "you (fsg) said to Yahweh" in v. 2 is quite strange. The context calls for a first person singular verb here and indeed this is how most of the early versions understood the passage.[1] Moreover, Dahood was correct to recognize Phoenician orthography here.[2] In Phoenician scribal practice final vowels were not indicated by *matres lectionis*, e.g., 1csg perfect verbs were written *ccct*,[3] so that *ʾmrt* would stand for "I said" as well as "you said." (It is difficult to explain why the Masora preserved *ʾāmart* here, except to suggest that the tradents knew it was not a 2msg form, that they did not consider the possibility of a 1csg form due to the lack of final *yod*, and that therefore the reading of a 2fsg form developed.) It is probable that Israelite scribes from the northern or northwestern border regions also employed Phoenician orthography and that the Bible occasionally has preserved such spellings.

The other attestations of this usage in the Bible are 1 Kgs 8:48, Ezek 16:59, Ps 140:13, Job 42:2, in all cases as Kethiv with the Qere reading -*tî*. With the exception of the second of these occurrences, this distribution confirms our conclusion. Based on the use of the Phoenician month names Ziv, Bul, and Ethanim in 1 Kgs 6:1, 6:37–38, 8:2, it is most likely that the description of the construction and dedication

---

[1] See Briggs, *Psalms*, 1.122, for a survey.

[2] Dahood, *Psalms I*, 87. Although he does not cite the parallel Phoenician usage, see also J. Lindblom, "Erwägungen zu Psalm xvi," *VT* 24 (1974) 190.

[3] Friedrich and Röllig, *Phönizisch-Punische Grammatik*, 58, 60.

of Solomon's Temple is the product of Phoenician scribes. In other words, not only did Phoenician architects and craftsmen build the Temple, their scribes also recorded the activity. Thus we can explain the orthography of 1 Kgs 8:48. Psalm 140 is a chapter replete with IH features, as will be discussed below (XIV.8). And the spelling in Job 42:2 should be added to the orthographic evidence adduced by Freedman in favor of the Israelian provenance of the book.[4]

3.   Twice in this psalm the feminine nominal ending *-āt* is preserved, in *mĕnāt* "portion" in v. 5 and in *naḥălāt* "heritage" in v. 6, as opposed to the standard Hebrew ending *-āh*. It is true that the first of these is in the construct state, but the vocalization *-āt*, with *qameṣ*, as opposed to *-at*, with *pataḥ*, indicates that this is a deviation from the JH norm. As noted above (I.4), forms with the ending *-āt*/*-at* appear disproportionately in northern contexts. Accordingly, the presence of two such nouns in Psalm 16 is a strong indication of the chapter's northern provenance.

4.   The root *nˁm* occurs twice in Psalm 16, in *nĕˁîmîm* "pleasant things" in v. 6 and in *nĕˁîmôt* "sweetness" in v. 11. This root is the normal word for "good, lovely, sweet, pleasant, etc." in Ugaritic and Phoenician.[5] As an indication of its common usage in Phoenician, I would point out that R. S. Tomback lists 13 occurrences of *nˁm* in his lexicon.[6] By comparison, in a much larger corpus of literature, note that *nˁm* occurs only 30 times in the Bible. Furthermore, *nˁm* is a fairly common element in Phoenician personal names.[7] In addition, *nˁmn* is the Phoenician name for Adonis,[8] and the same name is borne by one of the leading Aramean characters in the Bible, the general Naaman (2 Kings 5). All of this suggests that the root *nˁm* was common in areas to the north of Israel, Phoenicia in particular but perhaps Aram as well.

More importantly, of the 30 biblical occurrences of *nˁm*, a vast majority occur in texts where northern origin is likely. Nine times *nˁm*

----

    [4] Freedman, "Orthographic Peculiarities in the Book of Job."

    [5] For the Ugaritic documentation and for a general statement on *nˁm* in Ugaritic and Phoenician, see Gordon, *Ugaritic Textbook*, 445.

    [6] Tomback, *Phoenician and Punic*, 215–17. This work is only a dictionary, not a concordance of the Phoenician inscriptions. Additional instances of the root *nˁm* are to be found in the corpus of Phoenician and Punic epigraphic remains.

    [7] F. L. Benz, *Personal Names in the Phoenician and Punic Inscriptions* (Rome: Biblical Institute Press, 1972) 102, 146–47, 176, 185, 362.

    [8] See W. F. Albright, *Yahweh and the Gods of Canaan* (London: School of Oriental and African Studies, 1968) 186–87.

occurs in Proverbs, twice it appears in Song of Songs (1:16, 7:7), and once it is used in Job (36:11). It is attested ten times in Psalms. Of these, two are in our present chapter (16:6, 16:11), two are in Psalm 141 (vv. 4 and 6) to be treated below (XV.8), one occurs in the Asaph collection (81:3) (see below X.21), and one occurs in Psalm 133 (v. 1) also to be treated below (XIII.1).

Other instances of $n^c m$ also have northern connections. Gen 49:15 is Jacob's blessing to Issachar, one of the northern tribes. 2 Sam 23:1 recently has been demonstrated to be a northern composition.[9] Isa 17:10 appears in the address to Damascus and Ezek 32:19 appears in the address to Egypt, so that style-switching is likely in these two cases.[10] The remaining four usages of $n^c m$ are less likely to have northern affiliations, but even with these some ties may be possible. The two passages in David's lament over Saul and Jonathan (2 Sam 1:16, 1:26) are admittedly from the pen of a Judahite poet, but the setting is Gilboa and the two slain heroes are Benjaminites. Finally, the two cases in Zech 11:7, 11:10, are either to be explained as northern influence over post-Exilic Hebrew or as continuations of the address to Lebanon in 11:1–3. In other words, maximally 26 of 30 or minimally 22 of 30 usages of the root $n^c m$ in the Bible are in northern texts. I consider this a significant ratio. Coupled with the Phoenician and Ugaritic evidence, I conclude that $n^c m$ was commonly used in IH, and only very rarely employed in the dialect of Judah.

5. The word *šāprāh* in v. 6 represents one of only three uses of the root *špr* "good, pleasing, beautiful" in the Bible. The other two attestations are in Gen 49:21 and Job 26:13.[11] The former appears in Jacob's blessing to Naphtali, one of the northernmost tribes, and the latter appears in a book with much Aramaic coloring. In addition, the root *špr* is extremely common in Aramaic; it appears at Sefire, five times in Daniel, and frequently in post-Biblical Aramaic.[12] Based on its distribution in the Bible and the cognate usage in Aramaic, I conclude that the Hebrew root *špr* was an element of IH though not of JH.

---

[9] Rendsburg, "Northern Origin"; and Rendsburg, "Additional Notes."

[10] Given the close ties between Egypt and Byblos from at least the 3rd Millennium B.C.E., whatever Canaanite may have been known in Egypt was probably of the Phoenician dialectal type.

[11] I exclude the noun *šaprîrô* "his canopy (?)" in Jer 43:10, which may or may not be related to our root.

[12] Jastrow, *Dictionary*, 2.1619–20.

6. The noun *šĕmāḥôt* in v. 11 occurs only here and in Ps 45:16. Since the latter appears in another northern psalm (see below V.1), there is good reason to parse this vocable not as the plural of *simḥāh* "joy," but rather as a dialectal variation thereof.[13] Above (I.4) I noted that in most Canaanite dialects the feminine singular nominal ending -*at* was retained. This statement can be refined by noting that in Phoenician the ending was actually -*ōt*, because short *a* shifted to *ō*.[14] The form *šĕmāḥôt*, then, would be the northern Hebrew variant of standard *simḥāh*. This will be proved clearly for *šĕmāḥôt* in Ps 45:16, and it can be assumed for *šĕmāḥôt* in Ps 16:11 as well.

There are other nouns in the Bible which end in -*ôt* which are feminine singular and not feminine plural. An investigation of them leads to the conclusion that they too are northernisms. Here may be mentioned *ḥokmôt* "wisdom" in Prov 1:20, 9:1, and *ḥakmôt* "wise lady" in Judg 5:29, Prov 14:1, compositions with clear northern affinities[15]; *yĕdîdôt* "love" in Ps 45:1 (see below V.1); *yĕšûʿôt* "salvation" in Ps 53:7, which is the northern version of *yĕšûʿat* in Ps 14:7 (see below VII.1); *bĕhēmôt* "beast" in Ps 73:22 (where the context calls for a singular noun) (see below X.8); *ḥēmôt* "wrath" in Ps 76:11, Prov 22:24 (see below X.8); *ʿēdôt* "testimony" in Ps 132:12 (see below XII.6); and *hôlēlôt* "madness" in Qoh 1:17, 2:12, 7:25, 9:3.[16]

7. In v. 11 appears the parallel word-pair *śōbaʿ* "fullness" and *nĕʿîmôt* "pleasures." As Y. Avishur has pointed out, this pairing is unique in the Bible, but the two words are collocated as a syndetic parataxis four times in the Phoenician inscription of King Azitawadda (*KAI* 26 A I:6, II:7, II:12–13, II:16).[17] I consider this fact sig-

---

[13] Dahood (*Psalms I*, 91) was on the right track when he wrote "It may or may not be significant that the dis legomenon plural *šĕmāḥôt* occurs in highly Phoenicianizing contexts," but he did not carry this observation to its ultimate conclusion. M. Buttenweiser (*The Psalms* [Chicago: University of Chicago Press, 1938] 512) sensed that the word should be a singular. He translated it "joy" and called it an "intensive plural, intensifying the idea expressed—a nicety which is lost in the translation."

[14] Friedrich and Röllig, *Phönizisch-punische Grammatik*, 29–30, 106–7. The length of the *ō* vowel is unclear. For full discussion of all the pertinent data, notwithstanding a contrary conclusion, see A. Dotan, "Stress Position and Vowel Shift in Phoenician and Punic," *IOS* 6 (1976) 71–121.

[15] On Judges 5 see already Burney, *Judges*, 171–76. On Proverbs see above, p. 10.

[16] Rendsburg, "Morphological Evidence."

[17] Avishur, *Stylistic Studies of Word-Pairs*, 452, 461.

nificant and it may be added to our list of northern features exhibited by Psalm 16.

Summary

These seven elements of IH concentrated in a short poem of eleven verses are sufficient evidence for affirming the northern provenance of Psalm 16.[18] Dahood sensed this with his declaration that "the language and style are peculiarly Phoenician."[19] I would simply alter this judgment by stating that the chapter was written by a north Israelite poet whose Hebrew dialect included many isoglosses with Phoenician.

---

[18] A famous difficulty in Psalm 16, namely the spelling and vocalization of *tômîk* "maintain" in v. 5, could be solved by supposing that it represents the manner in which the active participle was pronounced in northern Israel. But there is no way of demonstrating this conclusively given the data available.

[19] Dahood, *Psalms I*, 87. Avishur (*Stylistic Studies of Word-Pairs*, 461) also noted that Psalm 16 "contains a large Canaanite, and especially Phoenician substrate."

CHAPTER III

Psalm 29

1. The primary clue for the northern provenance of Psalm 29 is the list of toponyms mentioned in the poem. This is not pure "linguistic evidence," to quote the title of this book, but it is very germane in the present instance. The poet mentions Lebanon and Sirion in vv. 5–6 and Qadesh in v. 8. The former two are the highest mountains in the region, in the far north of the territorial extent of the twelve tribes of Israel. The latter is not to be confused with Qadesh(-barnea) in Sinai, rather it refers to the Syrian Desert to the northeast of Israel. This has been discussed in detail by Ginsberg fifty years ago and by Dahood in his commentary.[1] The references to "cedars" in v. 5 and to "forests" in v. 9 also place us in the north, since these items are rare in Judah. Particular attention should be paid to the designation Sirion, instead of the usual biblical name Hermon. According to Deut 3:9 this term was used by the Sidonians. Presumably denizens of northern Israel also referred to the mountain as Sirion.

2. The phrase *běnê ʾēlîm* "sons of the gods" in v. 1 is what may be called a "double plural," that is, both the *nomen regens* and the *nomen rectum* of a construct chain are in the plural. Gevirtz recently has noted that this grammatical usage is characteristic of northern texts such as Judges 5, Phoenician inscriptions, and the Amarna letters from Byblos.[2] It is true that double plurals occur elsewhere in the

---

[1] See Ginsberg's works cited above, p. 13, n. 58; and Dahood, *Psalms I*, 178. I cannot accept the argument of Margulis ("The Canaanite Origin of Psalm 29 Reconsidered") that the poem has a southern orientation based on Qadesh = Qadesh-barnea and *ʾayyālôt* in v. 9 = Eloth/Elath.

[2] Gevirtz, "Of Syntax and Style in the 'Late Biblical Hebrew'—'Old Canaanite' Connection," 28–29; and Gevirtz, "Asher in the Blessing of Jacob (Genesis xlix 20)," 160.

Bible where northern provenance is not indicated, e.g., in Chronicles,[3] but the overall picture still favors Gevirtz's conclusion. Accordingly, the presence of this construction in Ps 29:1 can be adduced as part of the linguistic evidence supporting a northern provenance for this poem.

3. The usual plural of *ya'ar* "forest" is *yĕ'ārîm*, but in v. 9 the unique form *yĕ'ārôt* appears. The Ugaritic texts refer to a place named *y'rt*[4]; this suggests the possibility that in northern Canaan the plural of *ya'ar* took the ending *-ôt*, while further south the ending was *-îm*. [5]

4. Above (I.3) I opined that the use of *l* = "from" is a feature of IH. I also noted that one of the paradigm instances of this usage is Ps 29:10, where *yhwh lammabbûl yāšāb* means "Yahweh has reigned from (= since) the flood."[6]

5. In v. 11 we encounter the verbs *ntn* "give" and *brk* "bless" as parallel members. This word-pair occurs nowhere else in the Bible, but its cognates *ytn* and *brk* appear in syndetic parataxis in Phoenician (*KAI* 50:5).[7] As was the case above (II.7), I consider this fact significant and believe it may be utilized as another point in favor of the northern provenance of Psalm 29.

6. Ever since Ginsberg's seminal studies on Psalm 29, it has been apparent to all that this chapter shares more word-pairs with Ugaritic than any other biblical composition of similar length. This is not the place to present such a list—the data are well known.[8] However, I

---

[3]   See R. Polzin, *Late Biblical Hebrew: Toward an Historical Typology of Biblical Hebrew Prose* (HSM 12; Missoula, MT: Scholars Press, 1976) 42.

[4]   For references see Gordon, *Ugaritic Textbook*, 412.

[5]   See also Dahood, *Psalms I*, 179.

[6]   Ibid., 180.

[7]   Avishur, *Stylistic Studies of Word-Pairs*, 446. Furthermore, this may militate against the view expressed by many scholars that v. 11 is a gloss, added secondarily by the Israelite poet who adapted the presumed Canaanite original for Yahwistic purposes. For discussion see Margulis, "The Canaanite Origin of Psalm 29 Reconsidered," 345–46.

[8]   The most recent treatments of the subject, which deal not only with word-pairs but with all types of parallels between Ugaritic literature and Psalm 29, are Loretz, *Psalm 29: Kanaanäische El- und Baaltraditionen in jüdischer Sicht*; and Kloos, *YHWH's Combat with the Sea*, 13–124. See also Gaster, "Psalm 29," 55–65; Cross, "Notes on a Canaanite Psalm in the Old Testament," 19–21; and Cross, *Canaanite Myth and Hebrew Epic*, 151–56.

would suggest that this fact adds support to our argument for northern origin. Avishur has noted that the majority of "Biblical works, books and chapters that contain pairs common to them and Ugaritic, in a high degree of concentration [e.g., Hosea, Song of Songs, Psalm 29, Deuteronomy 32, Proverbs 1–9] . . . originate from the northern tribes."[9]

Summary

Even before the days of Ugaritic study, Gunkel had concluded that Psalm 29 was of northern origin. He based this assertion on the mention of Lebanon and Sirion.[10] Ginsberg's studies in the 1930's confirmed this view with a wealth of information forthcoming from the then newly discovered Ugaritic texts. The additional evidence garnered here corroborates this opinion.

---

[9] Avishur, *Stylistic Studies of Word-Pairs*, 440.
[10] Gunkel, *Psalmen*, 125.

CHAPTER IV

Psalm 36

1. In v. 2 is the difficult expression *nĕʾûm pešaʿ*.[1] As is well known, the word *nĕʾûm* generally is used when God is the speaker. Only in four contexts is it used with a human speaker: Numb 24:3–4, 24:15–16 with Balaam, 2 Sam 23:1 with David, Prov 30:1 with Agur, and here in Ps 36:2 in an admittedly obscure manner.[2] An examination of the first three instances indicates that *nĕʾûm* in connection with human speakers is a northern usage. Balaam stems from Pethor on the Euphrates in the land of Aram (Numb 22:5, Deut 23:5),[3] and his Hebrew is tinged with various Aramaisms.[4] The poem "The Last Words of David" in 2 Sam 23:1–7 includes no less than six IH elements in its seven verses (see above, p. 9). Similarly, Agur stems from Massa which, as noted above (I.6), is located by most authorities in the Syrian Desert.[5] Although Aramaisms may not be readily apparent in the verses attributed to him, in the passages ascribed to his congener Lemuel king of Massa, we may note such forms as *bar* "son" in Prov

---

[1] For detailed discussion see L. A. F. Le Mat, *Textual Criticism and Exegesis of Psalm XXXVI* (Utrecht: Kemink & Zoon, 1957) 4–8. However, I disagree with Le Mat's conclusion that *pešaʿ* needs to be revocalized to *pôšēaʿ*. This is also the solution of J. Leveen, "Textual Problems in the Psalms," *VT* 21 (1971) 55–56.

[2] This has been noted by W. Nowack, *Richter, Ruth und Bücher Samuelis* (HKAT; Göttingen: Vandenhoeck & Ruprecht, 1902) 251; Driver, *Notes on the Hebrew Text of the Books of Samuel*, 356; Le Mat, *Psalm XXXVI*, 4–5; and D. N. Freedman, "Divine Names and Titles in Early Hebrew Poetry," in *Magnalia Dei: The Mighty Acts of God: Essays on the Bible and Archaeology in Memory of G. Ernest Wright* (eds. F. M. Cross, W. E. Lemke, and P. D. Miller; Garden City, NY: Doubleday, 1976) 73 [reprinted in D. N. Freedman, *Pottery, Poetry, and Prophecy* (Winona Lake, IN: Eisenbrauns, 1980) 96].

[3] See S. E. Loewenstamm, "Bilʿām," *EM* 2 (1973) 133–34.

[4] For several examples see Rendsburg, "Northern Origin," 115–16.

[5] See above, p. 26 n. 34.

31:2 and *mĕlākîn* "kings" in Prov 31:3. Accordingly, the use of *nĕʾûm* in a non-divine context in Ps 36:2 is to be considered a northern feature.

2. In v. 6 we encounter the irregular form *bĕhaššāmayim* "in the heavens" with non-elision of the definite article (*h*) following a uniconsonantal prefixed preposition (*b, l, k*). This irregularity occurs elsewhere in the Bible in the following passages: 1 Sam 13:21, 2 Kgs 7:12K, Ezek 40:25, 47:22, Qoh 8:1, Neh 9:19, 12:38, 2 Chr 10:7, 25:10, 29:27.[6] The only parallel usage to the non-elision of *he* in this environment within the Canaanite sphere is its eightfold appearance in Punic.[7] Now it is true that this phenomenon does not occur in any standard Phoenician texts, but nevertheless we may suspect that it was native to some northern Canaanite dialects.[8] There are indications of this in at least some of the aforementioned biblical attestations.

In 1 Sam 13:21 the action occurs in the territory of Benjamin and the story concerns the kingship of Saul; 2 Kgs 7:12K is in the mouth of an Israelian king (which one is not altogether certain); Qoh 8:1 appears in a book where considerable northern influence has been demonstrated; and Neh 9:19 appears in a pericope which too originated in the northern kingdom.

I have only placed five of the eleven occurrences of this usage in northern texts, but proportionately this is sufficient to label this phenomenon a characteristic of IH.[9] The remaining six passages are all in exilic or post-exilic compositions. Here we may appeal to Gordon's hypothesis that late biblical literature evinces northern grammatical features due to the reunion of Israelian exiles and Judean exiles in Mesopotamia in the 6th Century B.C.E.

3. The expression *harĕrê ʾēl* "mountains of God" in v. 7 includes a reduplicatory plural of a noun based on a geminate stem.[10] Normally, Hebrew simply retains the gemination in such cases, e.g., *ʿām*

---

[6] I exclude from consideration 2 Sam 21:20, 21:22 *lĕhārāpāh* = 1 Chr 20:6, 20:8 *lĕhārāpāʾ*, where the *he* is apparently considered part of the title; Dan 8:16 *lĕhallāz* where the *he* is an essential part of the demonstrative pronoun; and the eight cases of *kĕhayyôm* "on this particular day" which is used to distinguish it from *kayyôm* "now."

[7] Friedrich and Röllig, *Phönizisch-punische Grammatik*, 53.

[8] See already R. C. Steiner, *The Case for Fricative-Laterals in Proto-Semitic* (AOS; New Haven: American Oriental Society, 1977) 43 and 55 n. 42.

[9] See also Rendsburg, "Northern Origin," 116; and Rendsburg, "Morphological Evidence."

[10] See Rendsburg, "Morphological Evidence."

"people," plural *ʿammîm*. But in a considerable number of instances the reduplicatory type appears, e.g., *ʿămāmîm*.[11] This latter method of forming the plural is standard in Aramaic, e.g., *ʿmmyʾ* "peoples," *kddn* "pitchers," *ṭllyʾ* "shades."[12] It will not be surprising to learn that a goodly number of the reduplicatory plurals in the Bible appear in texts where northern origin may be detected. This includes not a small number of instances of our word *harĕrê*.[13]

Numb 23:7 *harĕrê* "mountains of" is in the mouth of Balaam, the Aramean prophet (see above IV.1). Deut 33:15 *harĕrê* "mountains of" occurs in Moses' blessing to the tribe of Joseph. Judges 5, a poem of unquestionable northern origin, includes two reduplicatory plurals: *ʿămāmekâ* "your peoples" in v. 14 and *ḥiqĕqê* "decisions of" in v. 15. Ps 50:10 *harĕrê* "mountains of," Ps 76:5 *harĕrê* "mountains of," and Ps 77:18 *ḥăṣāṣekâ* "your arrows," all appear in the Asaph collection (see below X.3); Ps 87:1 *harĕrê* "mountains of" appears in the Korah collection (see below VI.12); and Ps 133:3 *harĕrê* "mountains of" occurs in a poem with northern connections (see below XIII.5).

Prov 29:13 *tekākîm* "oppressions" places us in a book with considerable northern influence.[14] Song 2:17, 4:6 *ṣĕlālîm* "shadows" and Song 4:8 *harĕrê* "mountains of" appear in a book with northern affinities. Nehemiah 9, whose northern provenience was mentioned earlier (p. 12) includes two such plurals: *ʿămāmîm* "peoples" in v. 22 and *ʿămĕmê* "peoples of" in v. 24. Finally, Jer 6:4 *ṣilĕlê* "shadows of" and Ezek 4:12, 4:15 *gelĕlê* "pellets of" appear in prophetic books where Aramaic influence may be increasingly seen and/or where IH influence had begun to show its effects due to the reunion of northerners and southerners in exile. Thus, we are left with only one occurrence which does not fit our interpretation: Hab 3:6.

---

[11] For the term "reduplicatory" and for the Afroasiatic background of this formation, see J. H. Greenberg, "Internal *a*-Plurals in Afroasiatic (Hamito-Semitic)," in *Afrikanistische Studien* (ed. J. Lukas; Berlin: Akademie Verlag, 1955) 198–204. In light of Greenberg's penetrating study, it is best to view the reduplicatory plurals of geminate nouns in Hebrew as internal or broken plurals with the *-îm* ending added secondarily due to *Analogiebildung*. Note the similarity between the Hebrew forms under discussion and such Afar-Saho (Cushitic) lexemes as *il* "eye," plural *ilal; boːr* "cloth," plural *boːrar*.

[12] Segert, *Altaramäische Grammatik*, 537, 546; and Jastrow, *Dictionary*, 1.537.

[13] The attempt by A. Robinson ("The Meaning of *ri* and the Dubiety of the Form *harre* and Its Variants," *VT* 24 [1974] 500–4) to emend many examples of *harĕrê* to *har rî* "mountain valley" is extremely weak and totally unconvincing.

[14] Furthermore, nearby in Prov 29:10 we encounter the expression *ʾanšê dāmîm* with both members of the construct chain in plural. On this construction as a northern element, see above III.2.

In short, we have isolated a grammatical feature which links Aramaic and IH,[15] and we can use the presence of *harêrê* in Ps 36:7 as another point in favor of our argument concerning this chapter's northern provenance. Although he did not approach the data from the same perspective, it is interesting to note that R. J. Tournay concluded similarly. He called the phrase *harĕrê ʾēl* "une expression superlative, d'origine phénicienne, qui évoque à l'origine le Liban."[16]

4.   Psalm 36 includes two examples of the retention of the *yod* in the inflection of III*y* verbs: *yeḥĕsāyûn* "seek refuge" in v. 8 and *yirwĕyûn* "overflowing" in v. 9. Many of the other examples of the non-elision of the *yod* in III*y* verbs, both perfect and imperfect, occur in sections of the Bible where northern origin may be detected or where code-switching is at work.[17] In addition, the retention of the *yod* in III*y* verbs is characteristic of Aramaic.[18]

The biblical forms which occur in northern compositions are Deut 32:37 *ḥāsāyû* "seek refuge," Ps 77:4 *ʾehĕmāyāh* "moan," Ps 78:44 *yištāyûn* "drink," Ps 83:3 *yehĕmāyûn* "moan," and Prov 26:7 *dalyû* "hang down." Also pertinent is the nominal form *maʾăwayyê* "desires of" in Ps 140:9. Deuteronomy 32 and Proverbs have been mentioned as northern compositions (see above, pp. 10, 12), three examples occur in the psalms of Asaph (see below X.4), and Psalm 140 is another northern poem (see below XIV. 3).

Code-switching is present in many other cases where the *yod* of III*y* verbs is retained, namely, Numb 24:6 *niṭṭāyû* "stretch out," Isa 17:12 *yehĕmāyûn* "roar," and Isa 21:12 *tibʿāyûn* "inquire," *bĕʿāyû* "inquire," *ʾētāyû* "come." The first occurs in the Balaam oracles with its Aramaizing tendencies, the second appears in Isaiah's address to Damascus, and the last three examples appear in Isaiah's reproduction of the speech of a watchman of Dumah.[19] In addition, we should

---

[15]   After I completed the research for this section, I was happy to discover that I was anticipated in my conclusion by E. Y. Kutscher, "Ha-Safa ha-ʿIvrit u-Venot Livyata be-Meshek ha-Dorot," *Hadoar* 47 (1968–69) 507–9 [reprinted in E. Y. Kutscher, *Hebrew and Aramaic Studies* (Jerusalem: Magnes, 1977) *šh-šṭw*].

[16]   R. J. Tournay, "Le Psaume XXXVI: Structure et Doctrine," *RB* 90 (1983) 13–14.

[17]   See Rendsburg, "Morphological Evidence."

[18]   See, e.g., *yhywn* "they will live" in line 8 of the inscription published by A. Caquot, "Une inscription araméene d'époque assyrienne," in *Hommages à Andre Dupont-Sommer* (Paris: Maisonneuve, 1971) 9–16. For the *yod* retaining consonantal force in some forms in Biblical Aramaic, see F. Rosenthal, *A Grammar of Biblical Aramaic* (Wiesbaden: Otto Harrassowitz, 1974) 51, 66.

[19]   See Kaufman, "Classification," 55; and Tur-Sinai, "ʾAramit," 593–94.

probably add the six examples from Job (3:25, 12:6, 16:22, 19:2, 30:14, 31:38), all of which are placed in the mouth of the protagonist.[20]

Summary

This psalm exhibits four grammatical usages which may be deemed characteristics of IH. This is clearly sufficient evidence for concluding that Psalm 36 stems from the northern regions of the land of Israel. Based on the expressions *harĕrê ʾēl* "mountains of El" and *tĕhôm rabbāh* "great deep" in v. 7, C. A. Briggs already opined that the author "was familiar with Lebanon and Hermon and the Mediterranean Sea, and possibly had his home in northwestern Galilee, where these were in view. The similes are so graphic that they could best be explained by an author standing on one of the summits of Lebanon, where all these things would come naturally into his mind."[21] The linguistic data presented above support this assumption.

Finally, it should be noted that occasional commentators have suggested that Psalm 36 is a composite of two separate compositions.[22] However, since the IH elements of this chapter span the proposed subdivisions, this approach is greatly weakened and the unity of the psalm is assured.[23]

---

[20] For the remaining few examples see the treatment by Robertson, *Linguistic Evidence*, 57–62. Robertson considered this feature to be an archaic element. In instances such as Exod 15:5, he is undoubtedly correct. I would trace the history of this form as follows. The retention of the *yod* in IIIy is used vestigially in EBH and perhaps in later archaizing poetry, but generally it disappears in SBH of the Judahite type. However, in IH this usage continues, as exemplified by the aforementioned cases.

[21] Briggs, *Psalms*, 1.315. For additional suggestions concerning a possible northern setting for this psalm, see Le Mat, *Psalm XXXVI*, 103–4, 106–7.

[22] For discussion see Briggs, *Psalms*, 1.314–20; and Kraus, *Psalmen*, 1.281.

[23] For additional arguments in favor of the psalm's unity, see Tournay, "Psaume XXXVI," 5–22.

CHAPTER V

Psalm 45

1. Above (II.6) I noted that the feminine singular nominal ending -ôt is a Phoenician form which no doubt was used in portions of northern Israel as well. Psalm 45 includes two examples of such nouns: yĕdîdôt in v. 1 and śĕmāḥôt in v. 16.[1] While it cannot be proved unequivocally that the former is feminine singular, to be translated "love," it is most probable. Tournay noted: "L'hébreu a un pluriel d'intensité; . . . Aquila suppose aussi le singulier."[2] Thus the expression śîr yĕdîdôt would mean "love song."[3]

The word śĕmāḥôt is linked with gîl in a hendiadys.[4] In such a construction there is typically number accord between the two components,[5] e.g., ḥesed wĕʾĕmet, ḥōq ûmišpāṭ, śar wĕśōpēṭ, but ḥuqqîm ûmišpāṭîm. The same is true of English hendiadys constructions: "by

---

[1] A third possible example is qĕṣîʿôt "cassia" in v. 9. R. Tournay ("Les affinités du Ps. xlv avec le Cantique des Cantiques et leurs interprétation messianique," *Congress Volume Bonn 1962* [SVT 9; Leiden: E. J. Brill, 1963] 191–92) noted that the noun itself is an Aramaic term, e.g., it occurs elsewhere only as qĕṣîʿāh in Job 42:14 as the name of Job's daughter in a non-Israelite context, and it is the Targumic rendering of Hebrew qiddāh in Exod 30:24. If this is correct, then the term may possibly be a northernism and the ending -ôt could possibly be a Phoenicianism. See also G. R. Driver, "Textual and Linguistic Problems of the Book of Psalms," *HTR* 29 (1936) 182.

[2] Tournay, "Affinités du Ps. xlv," 173 n. 1.

[3] See also the discussions by P. J. King, *A Study of Psalm 45 (44)* (Ph.D. dissertation, Pontificia Universitas Lateranensis, Rome, 1959) 46; and J. S. M. Mulder, *Studies on Psalm 45* (Ph.D. dissertation, Katholieke Universiteit te Nijmegen, 1972) 16.

[4] Buttenweiser, *Psalms*, 92. See also Mulder, *Studies on Psalm 45*, 136–37.

[5] This point has been made by E. Z. Melamed, "Shnayim shehem ʾeḥad (hen dia duoin) ba-Miqraʾ," *Tarbiz* 16 (1944–45) 173–89, especially p. 177. This article has been reprinted in *Miqraʾa be-Ḥeqer Leshon ha-Miqraʾ* (Liquṭe Tarbiz 3; ed. A. Hurvitz; Jerusalem: Magnes, 1982–83) 37–53.

hook or by crook," "jot and tittle," etc., vs. "odds and ends," "bits and pieces," etc. In Ps 45:16 since *gîl* is singular, then *šĕmāḥôt* must also be singular. Indeed the ancient versions are virtually unanimous in rendering *šĕmāḥôt* as a singular,[6] and many modern scholars do likewise.[7] As I noted earlier (II.6), by extension one will assume that *šĕmāḥôt* in Ps 16:11 is also singular.

2.   The verb *rḥš* "astir" in v. 2 occurs only here in the Bible. (The root also occurs in the noun *marḥešet* "saucepan" in Lev 2:7, 7:9.) The verb is well known from Aramaic.[8] Accordingly, this word represents an important lexical item linking IH and Aramaic. In Tournay's words: "Il est notable que le premier mot du psaume xlv soit un aramaïsme; d'autres vont aussi se rencontrer."[9]

3.   The term *māhîr* "skillful" in v. 2 has been widely discussed.[10] No one, however, has pointed out that it is non-Judahite in origin. The earliest attestation of this word is in the Egyptian text Papyrus Anastasi I, a satirical letter whose contents includes a virtual tour of much of the Levant. In fact the term is used exactly as in Ps 45:2, describing an efficient scribe.[11] Although the letter eventually leads to the southern sites Joppa and Gaza, it concentrates mainly in the north, mentioning such sites as Aleppo, Qadesh, Byblos, Beirut, Sidon, Sarepta, Hazor, Megiddo, etc.[12] Thus I consider it significant that the Egyptian author of this letter employed the term *mhr*.

Elsewhere in the Bible the word *māhîr* is used in Prov 22:29 in a work whose northern affinities are well established, in Ezra 7:6 (again in the expression *sôpēr māhîr*) where Aramaic influence is especially noteworthy, and in Isa 16:5 in an address to Moab. In extra-biblical literature it appears in Aramaic in the book of Ahiqar, column 1, line

---

6   See King, *A Study of Psalm 45 (44)*, 100.

7   See, e.g., T. H. Gaster, "Psalm 45," *JBL* 74 (1955) 251.

8   Jastrow, *Dictionary*, 2.1470.

9   Tournay, "Affinités du Ps. xlv," 175.

10   See, e.g., Tournay, "Affinités du Ps. xlv," 175–76; Mulder, *Studies on Psalm 45*, 86–87, 93; and E. Ullendorff, "The Contribution of South Semitics to Hebrew Lexicography," *VT* 6 (1956) 195.

11   I am not convinced by the argument of A. F. Rainey ("The Soldier-Scribe in *Papyrus Anastasi I*," *JNES* 26 [1967] 58–60) to disassociate Egyptian *šš mhr* from Hebrew *sôpēr māhîr*.

12   For the text, translation, and commentary see A. H. Gardiner, *Egyptian Hieratic Texts* (Leipzig, J. C. Hinrichs, 1911), especially pp. 20*–30*, 60–80. See also *ANET*, 475–479.

1, in the expression *spr ḥkym wmhyr* "a wise and excellent scribe."[13] In Ugaritic the root is used in the sense of "serviceman, soldier,"[14] which is semantically connected.[15] Finally, the root occurs as a component in the extremely common Phoenician-Punic personal name *mhrbᶜl*, and it is used in other such anthroponyms as well.[16] In other words, the attestations of the term *māhîr* or the root *mhr* (in instances where the meaning is "skilled" and not "speedy") are all in non-Judahite contexts. Its appearance in Ps 45:2 is thus explicable if we assume that this poem is a northern composition.

4.   The word *malkût* "kingdom" in v. 7 recalls the same Aramaic form, attested at Sefire and in later Aramaic. As is well known, the word becomes exceedingly common in Hebrew from the time of Jeremiah onward.[17] Earlier attestations of this word are limited to our present passage and to Numb 24:7 and 1 Kgs 2:12. The former places us once more in the Balaam oracles, where Aramaisms are expected. The latter is a bit more difficult to explain, though I would venture to suggest that it is written by an individual from northern Canaan, either Israelite or Phoenician.[18] The evidence points to *malkût* having been characteristic of IH at an early time, and only later did it penetrate to JH.

5.   Twice in this psalm the word *hêkāl* is used to mean "palace," as opposed to its usual meaning "temple,"[19] in the expressions *hêkĕlê šēn* "palaces of ivory" in v. 9 and *hêkal melek* "palace of the king" in v. 16. An examination of the other biblical usages of *hêkāl* = "palace" reveals this to be a northern idiom.

In 1 Kgs 21:1 the word is used to mean the palace of the Israelian king Ahab. The contexts of Hos 8:14 and Amos 8:3 imply that *hêkāl(ôt)* in these passages refers to royal palaces, not sacred temples.

---

[13]   A. E. Cowley, *Aramaic Papyri of the Fifth Century B.C.* (Oxford: Clarendon Press, 1923) 212, 226.

[14]   Gordon, *Ugaritic Textbook*, 431.

[15]   S. Morag, "ᶜIyyunim be-Yaḥase Mashmaᶜot," *Eretz-Israel* 14 (H. L. Ginsberg Volume) (1978) 137–47, especially pp. 138–40.

[16]   Benz, *Personal Names in the Phoenician and Punic Inscriptions*, 137–38, 340–41. See also Dahood, *Psalms I*, 271.

[17]   For discussion see Hurvitz, *Beyn Lashon le-Lashon*, 79–88. On its appearance in Ps 45:7 see in particular p. 88 and n. 49.

[18]   On Phoenicianisms in the description of Solomon's reign, see above, II.2. It is true that *malkût* is not a Phoenician term, but a similar form *mlkyt* does occur; see Tomback, *Phoenician and Punic*, 182.

[19]   BDB, 228; KB, 230–1.

This usage occurs in Joel 4:5 in a prophetic address to Tyre and Sidon. The expression *hêkĕlê melek* in Prov 30:28 occurs in a book with many Phoenician affinities, and in particular in a section between the two Massa segments (see Prov 30:1, 31:1). Elsewhere it refers to the palaces of either Babylonian or Assyrian kings (2 Kgs 20:18, Isa 13:22, 39:7, Nah 2:7, Dan 1:4, 2 Chr 36:7), a point which makes sense given the Mesopotamian origin of the Hebrew word *hêkāl* = Akkadian *ekallu* = Sumerian É.GAL. This leaves only Ps 144:12 where *hêkāl* = "palace," though this usage may be attributed to the presumed post-exilic date of this psalm.

The term *hkl/hykl* does not occur in Phoenician texts, but it does appear as an element in the personal name *grhkl*, which presumably means "resident of the palace" (as opposed to "resident of the temple"). In Ugaritic, the word *hkl* also means "palace." It is used in *UT* 1 Aqht:172 referring to the home of King Danel. In *UT* 33:9 it appears in a text which may refer to the royal family; note the expressions *ksu bᶜlt* "throne of the mistress (= queen?)" in l. 7 and *bt gdlt* "eldest daughter (= ranking princess?)" in l. 8. The other attestations of *hkl* are all in *UT* 51 in the famous description of the construction of a palace for Baal.

In short, both the internal biblical evidence and the cognate Phoenician and Ugaritic data point to the use of *hêkāl* for "palace" (as opposed to "temple") as a feature of northern Hebrew. Its twofold presence in Psalm 45 thus represents an important argument favoring the northern provenance of this poem. In addition, the expression *hêkĕlê šēn* suggests an Israelian context, for it was specifically in Samaria where "palaces of ivory" existed. This fact is known from the biblical passages 1 Kgs 22:39, Amos 3:15, and it has been confirmed by the archaeological excavations at Samaria.[20]

6.   The phrase *bĕnôt mĕlākîm* "daughters of kings" in v. 10 is another example of the double plural syntagma identified above (III.2) as a northern feature.

7.   The expression *bat ṣûr* "daughter of Tyre" in v. 13 is not technically a piece of linguistic evidence, and yet I mention it here because it obviously adds considerable weight to my argument.

8.   The form *yĕhôdûkā* "(peoples) shall praise you" in v. 18 runs counter to the norms of Hebrew grammar. Usually the *he* is elided

---

[20] See C. Decamps de Mertzenfeld, *Inventaire commenté des ivoires phéniciens et apparentés, découverts dans le Proche Orient, Texte* (Paris: E. de Boccard, 1954) 62–75.

after the preformatives of the Hiph^cil/Hoph^cal imperfect and participle (*yaqṭîl, maqṭîl,* etc.). In about ten instances, however, the *he* is retained. The same is true of the corresponding Aramaic Haph^cel,[21] a fact which led P. Joüon to suggest that the biblical examples were "peut-être en partie sous l'influence de l'araméen."[22] To some extent Joüon was correct, but some refinement of his position is necessary.

In two other instances in the Bible, Hiph^cil imperfects occur in poems where northern origin can be determined. Ps 116:6 *yĕhôšîa^c* occurs in a chapter in which other IH elements appear (see below XI.1), and the proper name *yĕhôsēp* "Joseph" in Ps 81:6 occurs in the Asaph collection (see below X.22). Six other examples of this formation occur in books from the time of Jeremiah to the time of Nehemiah (Isa 52:5, Jer 9:4, 37:3, Ezek 46:22, Job 13:9, Neh 11:17). For this set we may again appeal to Gordon's hypothesis concerning IH elements in postexilic literature or we may merely explain them as Aramaisms (*pace* Joüon). This leaves only two biblical attestations unexplained: 1 Sam 17:47 (in the mouth of David) and Ps 28:7 (in a chapter devoid of other IH elements).

I conclude, therefore, that the non-elision of *he* in Hiph^cil/Hoph^cal imperfects and participles is a northern feature which bridged Aramaic and IH.[23] The case of *yĕhôdûkâ* in Ps 45:18 can therefore be adduced as additional evidence concerning the northern provenance of this poem.

Summary

Previous scholars have argued that Psalm 45 is a northern composition based on its contents. Many consider it to be a Tyrian epithalamium in origin, adopted by the Israelites for the marriage of Ahab

---

[21] Segert, *Altaramäische Grammatik*, 264, 269; and Rosenthal, *A Grammar of Biblical Aramaic*, 44, 60.

[22] Joüon, *Grammaire de l'hébreu biblique*, 121.

[23] See Rendsburg, "Morphological Evidence." Robertson (*Linguistic Evidence*, 111) considered the retention of *he* in such forms an archaic feature of biblical poetry. To some extent he is correct, and perhaps this explains the examples of 1 Sam 17:47 and Ps 28:7. I would trace the history of this morpheme as follows. The non-elision of *he* in the Hiph^cil/Hoph^cal imperfects and participles is used vestigially in EBH. It disappears in SBH of the Judahite variety, but remains a feature of IH. Later, either under the influence of IH or Aramaic, it is reintroduced into LBH.

and Jezebel (note especially *bat ṣûr* in v. 13).[24] Briggs adduced some linguistic evidence, arguing that Aramaisms in the poem "might be explained from the dialect of North Israel, which was tending to the Aramaic earlier than the dialect of Judah, owing to proximity to Syria and constant association with Syrians in war and commerce."[25] Tournay also emphasized the fact that the chapter contains many Aramaisms.[26] Furthermore, Psalm 45 belongs to the group of Korah psalms, which as a unit also contains a significant concentration of IH elements (see below VI). In short, there can be little doubt that Psalm 45 is an Israelian composition.[27]

---

[24] See most importantly Buttenwieser, *Psalms*, 85–89. In an extremely illuminating study, Gaster ("Psalm 45," 239–51) pointed out "that in the Near East, as elsewhere, it is common convention to treat a bridal couple as royalty" (p. 239), thus it may be unnecessary to have to posit a particular royal couple as the subject of our poem. Although Gaster is correct, I would still argue for a northern provenance, based on the linguistic evidence presented above.

[25] Briggs, *Psalms*, 1.384. Some of his examples, however, are not altogether convincing. For example, Briggs suggested that the word *šēgal* "queen" in v. 10 "belongs to the dialect of the North." The noun occurs only here and in Neh 2:6. As a verb the root *šgl* occurs in decidedly Judahite contexts: Deut 28:30K, Isa 13:16K, Jer 3:2K, Zech 14:2K. I do not believe there is sufficient evidence here to defend Briggs' position, though one would not want to dismiss it outright either.

[26] Tournay, "Affinités du Ps. xlv," 172. See also Tournay's opinions cited in the discussions of the individual points above.

[27] J. P. J. Olivier ("The Sceptre of Justice and Ps. 45:7b," *JNSL* 7 [1979] 52–53) noted some similar expressions in Ugaritic and Phoenician to *šēbeṭ mîšōr* "scepter of equity" in v. 7. But since none of these parallels is an exact parallel, I refrain from utilizing this evidence to bolster my position.

CHAPTER VI

The Korah Psalms

Psalm 45 (see above V) belongs to the group of psalms ascribed to Korah. This collection comprises Psalms 42–49, 84–85, 87–88. Peters and Goulder hypothesized that the entire group originated in the north (see above p. 14). With the exception of Psalm 45, none of these chapters includes a high concentration of northern linguistic markers to affirm Israelian provenance. Nevertheless, taken as a group, there are indications of northern composition. Accordingly, I include here a chapter devoted to Psalms 42–44, 46–49, 84–85, 87–88.

1. We begin once more (as was the case with Psalm 29; see above III.1) with a non-linguistic argument, namely, the topographical setting of these chapters. Goulder has written: "The Korah series contains several references which read as though the water available were plentiful."[1] The following should especially be noted: Ps 42:7 "Therefore I recall you from the land of the Jordan," Ps 42:8 "The deep calls to the deep at the sound of your cataracts; all your breakers and waves pass by me," Ps 46:5 "The river, its streams gladden the city of God," Ps 87:7 "All my springs are in you," Ps 88:8 "With all your breakers you afflict me." The assumption is that a Judahite poet would not write in this manner, and that the region of the northern Jordan River valley would best fit these descriptions.

This is confirmed by the references to mountains in the Korah psalms; they too presume a northern location. In Ps 42:7 we read of ḥermônîm and har miṣʿār.[2] The former clearly refers to Mt. Hermon, and the plural form is to be explained due to this high mountain possessing several peaks. The latter was identified by G. Dalman as

---

[1] Goulder, *Korah*, 13–14.

[2] For discussion see F. Zorell, "Kritisches zu einigen Psalmversen," *Biblica* 7 (1926) 312–14.

zā'ōra, a place three miles south of Banias.[3] An objection to this conclusion was raised by H. Kruse, who wrote, "The present writer saw the source of the Jordan at Banyas (in September 1951) and found it a lovely place; but he was unable to discover the alleged 'roaring waterfalls' . . . and 'boisterous cataracts' which could have inspired the poet."[4] Consequently, Kruse stated, "The poet was, of course, living in Jerusalem."[5] However, on my own repeated visits to Banias (most recently in April 1987) I have been continually impressed with the waterfalls and cataracts which Kruse reported to have been unable to find. I should note that there are two tourist sites which include the name Banias. One is the nature reserve at the site of the ancient temple of Pan and the other is closer to Kibbutz Senir. At the former, it is true, the waters are quite tranquil; but at the latter are waterfalls and cataracts whose waters roar to the point of being almost deafening.

Ps 46:3–4 refers to the meeting of mountains and roaring and foaming seas. This only occurs in the north at places such as Carmel and Rosh Haniqra; in the south of course a wide coastal plain abuts the Mediterranean Sea.

In Ps 48:3 *yarkĕtê ṣāpôn* "the far north" is used as a synonym of Mt. Zion.[6] Whether this refers specifically to Mt. Saphon = Mt. Cassius near the Orontes River or whether it refers generally to the mountains of the north (Hermon, Lebanon, etc.) cannot be determined, but it is very likely that such a designation would have been coined by a northern poet.

Finally, there is the toponym *'ēmeq habbākā'* in Ps 84:7. This term has been the subject of much debate.[7] Generally scholars have sought to locate this valley by identifying it with the similar term *bĕkā'îm* in 2 Sam 5:23–24, thus placing it close to Jerusalem.[8] But there seems no *a priori* reason to do this. The best solution proposed has been Goul-

---

[3] G. Dalman, "Zu Psalm 42, 7. 8.," *PJB* 5 (1909) 101–3. This identification is accepted by Buttenweiser (*Psalms*, 231) and Kraus (*Psalmen*, 1. 320).

[4] H. Kruse, "Two Hidden Comparatives: Observations on Hebrew Style," *JSS* 5 (1960) 341.

[5] Ibid., 342.

[6] For discussion see P. L. Krinetzki, "Zur Poetik und Exegese von Ps 48," *BZ* 4 (1960) 86–88; Cross, *Canaanite Myth and Hebrew Epic*, 38 (where the reference to Ps 43:8 is a misprint for Ps 48:3); and A. Robinson, "Zion and *Saphon* in Psalm XLVIII 3," *VT* 24 (1974) 118–23.

[7] For succinct discussion see A. Robinson, "Three Suggested Interpretations in Ps. lxxxiv," *VT* 24 (1974) 378–79.

[8] See especially D. Yellin, "Emek Ha-Bakha: Bekhaim," *JPOS* 3 (1923) 191–92. W. Caspari ("Psalm 84 in drei Strophen," *ZDMG* 75 [1921] 54–55) even goes to the extent of emending Ps 84:7 to *habbĕkā'îm* on the basis of 2 Sam 5:23–24.

der's, which is to identify ʿēmeq habbākāʾ with the Galilean town of Baka mentioned by Josephus (*War* 3.3.1). This site "lies at the head of a dry valley running down to the sea at Accho,"[9] thus matching the description of Ps 84:7 as "the valley of Baka."[10] Moreover, Papyrus Anastasi I, column 23, line 7, mentions the *b3k3*-tree specifically in connection with the tribe of Asher.[11]

These passages have led several commentators to suggest a northern setting for the Korah poems. Briggs wrote concerning Psalm 42: "Mount Hermon and the sources of the Jordan seem to be the place of sojourn of the poet. . . . The internal evidence points to a [poet] who was especially at home in the regions of the upper Jordan and Mount Hermon."[12] Concerning Psalm 46 he wrote: "The author was familiar with the effects of an earthquake on mountains and sea, probably at the base of Mt. Carmel."[13] To this Dahood added: "The imagery would readily spring to mind along the Phoenician littoral where the Lebanon Mountains in many places begin their rise at the edge of the Mediterranean waters."[14]

2. In 42:2 we have one of the clearest examples of a 3msg imperfect with *t*- preformative: *kěʾayyāl taʿărōg* "as the hart thirsts." There has been some debate as to whether BH specifically or Northwest Semitic generally admits such a grammatical feature.[15] I side with those scholars who believe that a few passages do reflect this usage. Here I would affirm Job 18:14, 18:15, 20:9, all noted by Sarna,[16] and Qoh 10:15 and our verse Ps 42:2, both noted by van Dijk.[17] In extra-biblical

---

[9] Goulder, *Korah*, 40. Robinson ("Three Suggested Interpretations in Ps. lxxxiv," 379) wrote as follows: "If there was, indeed, such a valley it was probably dry and waterless in the summer. The parallelism demands this and it is, therefore, fair to translate 'a desert valley.'"

[10] If the term is to be connected with the Hebrew root *bkh* "cry," note that *habbākkāʾ* in Ps 84:7 with final *aleph* is "une graphie aramaïsante"; thus R. Tournay, "Les psaumes complexes," *RB* 54 (1947) 525. This would be additional support for our northern hypothesis.

[11] See Gardiner, *Egyptian Hieratic Texts*, 25*, 70.

[12] Briggs, *Psalms*, 1.367.

[13] Ibid., 1.394.

[14] Dahood, *Psalms I*, 279.

[15] Proponents are N. M. Sarna, "The Mythological Background of Job 18," *JBL* 82 (1963) 317–18; and H. J. van Dijk, "Does Third Masculine Singular **taqtul* Exist in Hebrew?" *VT* 19 (1969) 440–7. Opponents are W. L. Moran, "**taqtul*—Third Masculine Singular?" *Biblica* 45 (1964) 80–82; and Ratner, *Gender Problems in Biblical Hebrew*, 57–62.

[16] Sarna, "The Mythological Background of Job 18," 317–18.

[17] Van Dijk, "Third Masculine Singular **taqtul*," 444–45.

material I would point to *KAI* 1:2, pointed out by Z. Harris,[18] and El Amarna letters 71:5 (Byblos), 86:4 (Byblos), 143:27 (Beirut), 323:22 (Ashkelon), all described by E. Ebeling.[19] It is noteworthy that none of these is in a Judahite context. As we have noted before, Job appears to be written in a Transjordanian dialect and Qohelet also reflects IH. The Phoenician and Amarna attestations also place us in the north (or in one instance in Ashkelon along the coast). Accordingly, I conclude that BH does admit a 3msg *t-* preformative, but that it is limited to regional variation.

3.   Four times in the Korah psalms the plural form *miškĕnôt* "tabernacles" appears,[20] in 43:3, 49:12, 84:2, 87:2.[21] In two of these instances (43:3, 84:2) the meaning is in fact singular.

The plural term is used elsewhere in the Bible in the following passages: Numb 24:5, Isa 32:18, 54:2, Jer 9:18, 30:18, 51:30, Hab 1:6, Ps 78:28, 132:5, 132:7, Job 18:21, 21:28, 39:6, Song 1:8. The first of these is in the Balaam oracles; Jer 51:30 and Hab 1:6 are in the context of Babylon/Chaldea; Psalm 78 is part of the Asaph collection (see below X.13); Psalm 132 is also a northern poem (see below XII.3); the three Job passages place us in a Transjordanian setting; and Song of Songs is also an Israelian composition. This leaves only four occurrences of this form (Isa 32:18, 54:2, Jer 9:18, 30:18) in decidedly Judahite contexts; and one of these (Isa 54:2) is Exilic.

The singular connotation of *miškĕnôt* is also apparent in Ps 78:28, 132:5, 132:7, Isa 54:2, Job 18:21, 39:6, and perhaps Song 1:8.[22] All of these are in Israelian settings, with the exception of Isa 54:2, which may be explained according to the theory of the reunion of northern and southern exiles in Babylon.

As several scholars have recognized, the singular meaning of Hebrew *miškĕnôt* is paralleled in Ugaritic usage,[23] in *UT* 128:III:19, 2 Aqht

---

[18] Z. Harris, *A Grammar of the Phoenician Language* (AOS 8; New Haven, CT: American Oriental Society, 1936) 65.

[19] E. Ebeling, "Das Verbum der El-Amarna-Briefe," *BASS* 8 (1910) 46, 48, 51.

[20] In the discussion which follows, I cite the form only as *miškĕnôt*, the plural construct. In most of the passages it appears with pronominal suffixes and occasionally it appears as *miškānôt*, the plural absolute.

[21] See Goulder, *Korah*, 3.

[22] On the last passage specifically and for general discussion, see Pope, *Song of Songs*, 333–34.

[23] The phenomenon in Ugaritic was first noted, as far as I can determine, by C. H. Gordon, "The Poetic Literature of Ugarit," *Orientalia* 12 (1943) 74. It has been applied to the Hebrew evidence by Tournay, "Les psaume complexes," 523; and by Dahood, *Psalms I*, 262.

V:32–33.[24] This confirms our interpretation that *miškĕnôt* is a northern usage, either regardless of connotation or specifically with singular meaning. For the related issue of the form *miškĕnê*, an alternative plural construct, see below VI.6.

4. The root *p⁽l* "do, make, work" appears in Ps 44:2, as opposed to the typical Hebrew verb *⁽śh*. As is well known, *p⁽l* is standard in Phoenician[25] and Ugaritic uses the by-form *b⁽l*.[26] Furthermore, *p⁽l* is now attested in the Deir ⁽Alla texts (Combination I, line 2).[27] In none of these languages, in fact, does the verb *⁽śy* occur.[28] Accordingly, the presence of *p⁽l* in a Hebrew composition may be an indication of northern provenance. And while not all attestations of Hebrew *p⁽l* appear in non-Judahite texts, a significant proportion of them occurs in works such as the Balaam oracles, Hosea, Proverbs, and Job.[29] I conclude, therefore, that the appearance of *p⁽l* in a biblical text is on its own not sufficient for positing northern origin. Yet, it was undoubtedly a feature of IH. Thus, when other IH characteristics are present in a particular composition, the use of *p⁽l* may be advanced to bolster the argument for northern provenance.

5. As noted by Dahood,[30] Ps 46:3 *lō³ nîrā³ bĕhāmîr ³āreṣ* "we are not afraid of the changing of the earth," and Ps 49:6 *lāmmāh ³îrā³ bîmê rā⁽* "why should I fear the days of evil," are two of only three instances in the Bible where the verb *yr³* governs the preposition *b*. The only other place is Jer 51:46, but since this appears in the prophet's long address to Babylon, one could explain this example as the result of code-switching. In the vast majority of instances, the verb *yr³* governs

---

[24] For an analysis of these passages see Avishur, *Stylistic Studies of Word-Pairs*, 343–44.

[25] Tomback, *Phoenician and Punic*, 267–68.

[26] Gordon, *Ugaritic Textbook*, 375.

[27] See J. A. Hackett, *The Balaam Text from Deir ⁽Allā* (HSM 31; Chico, CA: Scholars Press, 1980) 25, 34–35.

[28] The Ugaritic word *⁽śy* seems to have specified meanings. In *UT* 2 Aqht I:30; 48, II:19, VI:8, it may mean "do evil." In *UT* 1079:7, 10, it may mean "fertile." See Gordon, *Ugaritic Textbook*, 462.

[29] I exclude from my calculations the construct plural participle *pō⁽ălê* which is quite frequent in the idiom *pō⁽ălê ³āwen*, and the noun *pō⁽al* "labor, work," which likewise is a common word in the Bible. For similar purposes, A. Hurvitz ("Linguistic Criteria for Dating Problematic Biblical Texts," *Hebrew Abstracts* 14 [1973] 75) excluded *pō⁽ălê ³āwen* from his investigations.

[30] Dahood, *Psalms I*, 278.

the preposition *m(n)*.[31] The use of *b* in place of *m(n)* (see above I.3) in these two passages in the Korah collection is additional evidence favoring a northern origin for these psalms.

6. Above (VI.3) we noted that the form *miškĕnôt* "tabernacles" appears disproportionately in Israelian literature. An alternative plural construct form *miškĕnê* occurs in Ps 46:5. The only other attestation of this usage is Ezek 25:4,[32] in the prophet's address to Ammon, where style-switching appears to be operating. Although we have no extrabiblical material by which to substantiate our supposition, the innerbiblical evidence points to the conclusion that the form *miškĕnê* is an IH feature.

7. A number of feminine nouns ending in *-ôt* in these chapters are not to be treated as plural, rather as feminine singular forms (see above II.6). In Ps 49:4 it seems probable that both *ḥokmôt* "wisdom" and *tĕbûnôt* "understanding" are to be treated as singular.[33] Ps 49:12 *'ădāmôt* appears only here in the Bible; it must mean "earth" in the singular and not "lands" in the plural.[34] Finally, there seems little doubt that Ps 88:9 *tôʿēbôt* is to be understood as singular "abomination," as the context clearly dictates.[35]

---

[31] BDB, 431.

[32] See Goulder, *Korah*, 3, where, however, Ezek 37:27 is incorrectly cited. MT here has *miškānî* "my tabernacle."

[33] This was understood by Briggs (*Psalms*, 1.412) and by E. Podechard ("Notes sur les Psaumes: Psaume XLIX," *RB* 31 [1922] 8), though these two scholars did not advance the argument of northern dialectal trait; and by Albright ("Some Canaanite-Phoenician Sources of Hebrew Wisdom," 8) and Dahood (*Psalms I*, 296–97), who did understand the usage as an IH feature. This militates against the suggestion of J. van der Ploeg, "Notes sur le Psaume xlix," in *Studies on Psalms* (OTS 13; Leiden: E. J. Brill, 1963) 143. Concerning *ḥokmôt* he wrote: "C'est dans ce dernier sens que le pluriel (rare et poétique) est employé ici." See similarly A. Cohen, *The Psalms* (London: Soncino Press, 1945) 152: "Both words are in the plural to denote profound wisdom and deep insight." For a survey of additional opinions see P. Casetti, *Gibt es ein Leben vor dem Tod?* (OBO 44; Göttingen: Vandenhoeck & Ruprecht, 1982) 266.

[34] Thus Dahood, Psalms I, 299; and Casetti, *Gibt es ein Leben vor dem Tod?*, 77. Van der Ploeg ("Psaume xlix," 151) sensed the correct meaning, and stated that the word reflects "le même sens que le singulier *'ădāmāh* et fait allusion à Gen. iii 19." However, he still called *'ădāmôt* "un pluriel solennel et poétique." For further discussion see P. Volz, "Psalm 49," *ZAW* 55 (1937) 255–56.

[35] M. Dahood, *Psalms II* (AB 17; Garden City, NY: Doubleday, 1968) 305. Briggs (*Psalms*, 2.249) stated, "pl. seems unncessary," and noted that the LXX and the Vulgate both interpreted the word as singular.

8. The negative particle *bal* appears twice in these chapters, at Ps 46:6, 49:13 (see above I.5).

9. The double plural *nĕdîbê ʿammîm* "princes of the peoples" occurs in Ps 47:10 (on this feature see above III.2). Contrast the same expression with Numb 21:18 *nĕdîbê hāʿām* and Ps 113:8 *nĕdîbê ʿammô* with the *nomen rectum* in the singular.[36]

10. At the outset I stated my aversion to emending MT, especially when linguistic arguments are being made. But I also mentioned some exceptions to this position. One such case is *passĕgû* in Ps 48:14. A root *psg* is rare in Semitic, besides which none of its attested meanings fits the context of Ps 48:14.[37] The proper solution to this crux seems to be that of Dahood, who analyzed consonantal *psgw* as the conjunction *p* and the imperative plural of the root *swg* "fence about."[38] This verb fits the context of the passage nicely. More to the point of our present undertaking, it needs to be pointed out that the conjunction *p* is a feature of IH. Except for its presence in Arabic in a more distant branch of the Semitic languages, this form is known from Ugaritic, Samalian, and Aramaic, all used to the north or northeast of the land of Israel.[39] The one other place in the Bible where this form can be reconstructed with relative assurance, namely, Ps 50:10, is also in a northern poem (see below X.2).

11. Based on both its nominal formation and its distribution in biblical literature, the word *yĕqār* in Ps 49:13, 49:21 has been considered an Aramaism by scholars.[40] Elsewhere it occurs only in Jeremiah, Ezekiel, Zechariah, Proverbs, Job, and Esther. Moreover, with the specific meaning "honor," which it possesses in Ps 49:13, 49:21, it oc-

---

[36] See also Ginsberg, *Israelian Heritage*, 34.

[37] For a convenient summary of the data and scholarly opinions, see F. E. Greenspahn, *Hapax Legomena in Biblical Hebrew* (SBLDS 74; Chico, CA: Scholars Press, 1984) 151.

[38] M. Dahood, "The Language and Date of Psalm 48 (47)," *CBQ* 16 (1954) 17–18. In a later treatment Dahood (*Psalms I*, 293) proposed the root *syg* as a by-form of *śyg* "examine, meditate," but this is less probable than the root *swg*.

[39] For specific references see Gordon, *Ugaritic Textbook*, 465; and Garr, *Dialect Geography*, 114–15.

[40] E. Kautzsch, *Die Aramaismen im Alten Testament* (Halle: M. Niemeyer, 1902) 38; Podechard, "Psaume XLIX," 13; Wagner, *Aramaismen*, 62–63; R. Gordis, *The Book of Job* (New York: Jewish Theological Seminary, 1978) 307; and Casetti, *Gibt es ein Leben vor dem Tod?*, 86.

curs again only in Esther and in the Aramaic portions of Daniel.[41] Based on the approach taken in the present article, I would slightly modify this opinion. The presence of *yĕqār* "honor" in Ps 49:13, 49:21, is not due to true Aramaic influence, rather it represents a feature shared by IH and Aramaic. (See similarly above II.5, V.2 and below VI.15.)

12. The plural form *harĕrê* "mountains of" in Ps 87:1 is the reduplicatory type which has already been described as an IH element (above IV.3).

13. The phrase *yhwh yispōr biktôb ʿammîm* in Ps 87:6 is surely to be translated as "Yahweh will count in the register of peoples," and not as the meaningless "Yahweh will count in the writing of the peoples."[42] Accordingly, the word *kĕtôb* here equals standard BH *kĕtāb* (Ezek 13:9, Ezra 2:62, Neh 7:64, etc.). As Dahood noted, the former is simply the northern form with short *a* having shifted to *o* (= Masoretic /ō/, a tone-long vowel [as opposed to a pure long vowel /ô/]).[43] This has been discussed above (II.6) in conjunction with the fsg ending *-ôt*.

14. The term *māḥălat*, the name of a musical instrument, in Ps 88:1, retains the absolute fsg ending *-at*, identified above (I.4) as an element of IH.

15. The verb *dwr* "dwell" appears in the Bible only at Ps 84:11. Briggs identified it as an Aramaism,[44] based on its more common appearance in Aramaic.[45] In more accurate terminology, I would now restate the issue: the verb represents an isogloss linking IH and Aramaic. See similarly above II.5, V.2, VI.11.

---

[41] BDB, 430, 1096.

[42] Such a translation would parse *biktôb* as the infinitive construct of *ktb* with prefixed *b-*; see Briggs, *Psalms*, 2.242; and A. Vaccari, "Note critiche ed esegetiche," *Biblica* 28 (1947) 396.

[43] Dahood, *Psalms II*, 300. There is no need to emend MT to *kĕtāb* as conjectured by KB, 460; and BHS, ad loc.

[44] Briggs, *Psalms*, 2.230. See also Wagner, *Aramaismen*, 43–44.

[45] See, e.g., Jastrow, *Dictionary*, 1.288.

Summary

The repeated mention of abundant water and lofty mountains led scholars to opine that some if not all of the Korah psalms were written by northern poets. Characteristics of individual poems in the collection led other scholars to the same conclusion. For example, Ginsberg noted many connections between Psalm 47 and the book of Amos.[46] M. Weiss came very close to claiming a non-Judahite authorship for Psalm 46 by noticing "the striking and characteristic fact that our psalm does not mention either 'Jerusalem' or 'Zion.'"[47] Dahood added a linguistic comment regarding Psalm 49: "the language is probably the most dialectal in the Psalter."[48] And J. Morgenstern believed that Psalm 48 was a pilgrimage psalm for worshippers en route to Jerusalem. More precisely, he stated, "The identification of Mount Zion with *yarkete Ṣafon* . . . suggests that these pilgrims in all likelihood came from the north, most probably from Galilee. It is undoubtedly a Galilean pilgrimage psalm, precisely as Ps. 42–43 unmistakably is."[49]

As stated at the outset of this section, with the exception of Psalm 45, no single psalm in the Korah group has a concentration of grammatical features which would mark it as a northern composition. Yet the collection as a whole includes enough such elements to demonstrate the basic validity of Peters' and Goulder's claim that these chapters originate in the north[50] and were only later transferred south to Jerusalem (see above p. 14).[51]

---

[46] Ginsberg, *Israelian Heritage*, 33–34. On the other hand, Ginsberg (p. 31) was equally confident of a Judahite origin for Psalms 46 and 48.

[47] M. Weiss, *The Bible From Within: The Method of Total Interpretation* (Jerusalem: Magnes, 1984) 330, see also p. 349.

[48] Dahood, *Psalms I*, 296.

[49] Morgenstern, "Psalm 48," 93.

[50] Thus the linguistic evidence militates against the view of J. M. Miller ("The Korahites of Southern Judah," *CBQ* 32 [1970] 58–68) that these psalms originate in the Hebron-Arad area. On the other hand, from their content Miller did adduce the fact that the Korah psalms were not written in Jerusalem.

[51] There are two other items in the Korah psalms which may be considered northern, but the evidence is not conclusive. The first is the lexeme *šīrōh* in Ps 42:9. T. H. Gaster ("Psalm 42:8," *JBL* 73 [1954] 237–38) identified this word with Ugaritic *drt* and translated it "his vision," and this opinion was accepted by Dahood (*Psalms I*, 259). For the Ugaritic word, see Gordon, *Ugaritic Textbook*, 388. For the equation of Ugaritic *d* and Hebrew *š*, see Pope, *Song of Songs*, 33. While this remains a possibility, it is by no means a sure equation. However, if this view is accepted, it would be an additional IH element in the Korah collection.

The second usage is the expression *ʾēl ḥāy* "the living God" in Ps 42:2, 84:3. Elsewhere in the Bible this phrase appears in Josh 3:10, Hos 2:1, and in a modified form in Amos 8:14. See Goulder, *Korah*, 3, 15. The two prophetic occurrences are, of course, in the northern prophets. Thus only the Joshua passage appears to be Judahite, though even here the story is geographically set in the territory of Benjamin (at the Jordan near Jericho) and of course Joshua himself would have been an Ephraimite tribal hero. The concept of "the living God" has a near parallel in the Ugaritic texts, where the word *ḥy* is predicated of Baal in several important passages (see especially *UT* 49:III:2, 8, 20). Both the distribution of the expression and the extra-biblical evidence point to *ʾēl ḥāy* being an Israelian feature. But because the phrase is so generic in meaning, and because it is not that widely attested, and because the Ugaritic and biblical texts do not correspond exactly, I hesitate incorporating *ʾēl ḥāy* into the above list of IH elements in the Korah psalms. (Note, for example, the very similar words *ʾĕlōhîm ḥāy* expressed by Hezekiah in 2 Kgs 19:4, 19:16 = Isa 37:4, 37:18.) The door remains open, nonetheless, for future discoveries to yield a more conclusive position.

CHAPTER VII

Psalm 53

1. Psalm 53 is obviously a duplicate of Psalm 14.[1] Dahood has already stated that the former is a northern variation of the latter.[2] The most telling indication of this is the use of *yĕšûʿ ôt* in Ps 53:7, corresponding to *yĕšûʿ at* in Ps 14:7. The former is not the plural, rather the feminine singular (in this case construct) ending in *-ôt* (see above II.6).[3]

2. The superscription in Ps 53:1 includes the term *māḥălat*, which is wanting in Ps 14:1. This noun form, with the feminine singular ending *-at*, would be characteristic of northern Hebrew (see above I.4).

Summary

Admittedly these two data represent slender evidence on which to build a hypothesis concerning the northern origin of Psalm 53. Indeed, if we did not possess Psalm 14, we would not arrive at such a conclusion. But the point is that we do have the two psalms, and Dahood's view seems justified.[4]

---

[1] For a convenient comparison of the two psalms, with side-by-side placement, see A. Bendavid, *Maqbilot ba-Miqraʾ* (Jerusalem: Carta, 1972) 210–11. The differences between the two versions are also collated by S. Weissblit, "Tehillim Mizmor 14 ve-ha-Maqbil Lo 53," *Beth Miqra* 29 (1983–84) 133.

[2] Dahood, *Psalms I*, 81; and Dahood, *Psalms II*, 19.

[3] Those scholars who try to reconstruct the *Urtext* of these duplicate psalms uniformally choose the form *yĕšûʿ at* over *yĕšûʿ ôt*. See, e.g., C. C. Torrey, "The Archetype of Psalms 14 and 53," *JBL* 46 (1927) 192; and K. Budde, "Psalm 14 und 53," *JBL* 47 (1928) 182. Apparently E. G. King ("On the Text of Psalms XIV and LIII," *Hebraica* 2 [1885–86] 237–39) did not consider v. 7 of these two psalms to be an original part of the poem.

[4] Our conclusion parallels the opinion of A. Jirku, "Doppelte Überlieferungen im Mythus und im Epos von Ugarit?" *ZDMG* 110 (1960) 20–25. He argued that

the variations in parallel texts in Ugaritic literature are to be ascribed to different regional dialects.

CHAPTER VIII

Psalm 58

1. The word ʿôlôt in v. 3 is obviously not the feminine plural participle of the verb ʿlh "go up." Rather, as almost all commentators and translations understand it, it is a variant of ʿawlāh and is to be translated "iniquity, evil, wickedness, etc."[1] Indeed this is how the Septuagint, Peshitta, and Targum already render ʿôlôt. Accordingly, Dahood's analysis is correct: "Masoretic ʿōlōt is the Phoenician pronunciation of classical Heb. ʿawlāh, 'injustice, malice.' In Phoenician, the diphthong of the first syllable aw contracts to ō (Friedrich, PPG, § 86), while the Hebrew feminine ending -āh appears in Phoenician as -ōt. Hence ʿōlōt is the genuine Phoenician form of Heb. ʿawlāh"[2]

2. The root pʿl "do, make, work" appears in v. 3. As argued above (VI.4), in a composition with other elements of IH, the presence of this verb may be put forward as additional support in favor of the northern origin of this psalm.

3. Also appearing in v. 3 is the verb pls "weigh, make level, straighten." This root is relatively rare in Hebrew, but it appears more commonly in Northwest Semitic languages used to the north of Israel. In Phoenician it appears as a noun meaning "architect"[3] and it is a common element in personal names.[4] It also appears in Ugaritic

---

[1] Thus Briggs, *Psalms*, 2.42; Buttenweiser, *Psalms*, 766; JPSV; etc.

[2] Dahood, *Psalms II*, 58. Accordingly, the slight alteration of MT to read ʾāwel, with the assumption of a double writing of the t based on the fact that the next word begins with the same consonant, is unnecessary. Thus, for example, Kraus, *Psalmen*, 1.415.

[3] Tomback, *Phoenician and Punic*, 264–65.

[4] Benz, *Personal Names in the Phoenician and Punic Inscriptions*, 73, 97, 140–41, 176, 391.

and Amorite personal names.[5] Its distribution in the Bible correlates with these northern affinities. Besides Ps 58:3, *pls* appears in Proverbs 1–9 three times (4:26, 5:6, 5:21), in the Asaph collection of Psalms (78:50) (see below X.16), and in Isa 26:7. Only the last of these texts is Judahite in nature; the remainder all have Israelian connections.

4.   The noun *ḥēmāh* "venom, poison" occurs twice in v. 5. The only other attestations of this word in the Bible are all in northern texts: Deut 32:24, 32:33, Ps 140:4, Job 6:4.[6] Deuteronomy 32 and the book of Job do not require further comment. On Ps 140:4 see below XIV.2. The cognate form *ḥmt* occurs repeatedly in the two snake charms found at Ugarit, texts RS 24.244 and RS 24.251,[7] thus confirming the northern usage of this word.

5.   The noun *peten* "viper, serpent" appears in v. 5. From the cognates Ugaritic *bṯn* and Arabic *baṯan*, it is clear that standard Hebrew would have *šin* as the middle root letter of this word.[8] Instead, *peten* appears with *taw*, exactly as is the case in Aramaic: Sefire *btn*,[9] Jewish Aramaic and Syriac *patna*. Scholars have been too quick to label Hebrew *peten* an Aramaism.[10] The correct interpretation is that of W. F. Albright, who described *peten* as "borrowed from a dialectal form like Aram. *patna*."[11] This dialect would be a northern Hebrew dialect in which *ṯ* shifted to *t*, as in Aramaic, and not to *š*, as in standard Hebrew.[12] In fact, as Albright also discovered, the standard reflex of our

---

[5] Gordon, *Ugaritic Textbook*, 468; F. Gröndahl, *Die Personennamen der Texte aus Ugarit* (Rome: Pontifical Biblical Institute, 1967) 172–73; and H. B. Huffmon, *Amorite Personal Names in the Mari Texts* (Baltimore: Johns Hopkins Press, 1965) 255.

[6] In none of these cases does the singular absolute *ḥēmāh* actually occur. Rather the attestations are always singular construct forms.

[7] The texts are treated in detail by M. C. Astour, "Two Ugaritic Serpent Charms," *JNES* 27 (1968) 13–36.

[8] The interchange between initial *b* and *p* in the various cognates has little effect on our discussion. The same holds for the variation between final *n* and final *m* in the Akkadian form *bašmu*.

[9] J. A. Fitzmyer, *The Aramaic Inscriptions of Sefire* (Rome: Pontifical Biblical Institute, 1967) 49. As Fitzmyer noted, this form also evinces the *b/p* interchange.

[10] Wagner, *Aramaismen*, 97; and N. H. Tur-Sinai, *The Book of Job* (Jerusalem: Kiryath Sepher, 1957) 313.

[11] W. F. Albright, "A Catalogue of Early Hebrew Lyric Poems (Psalm LXVIII)," *HUCA* 23/1 (1950–51) 27. For an earlier discussion see W. F. Albright, "New Light on Early Canaanite Language and Literature," *BASOR* 46 (1932) 19 n. 16.

[12] This parallels the development of the root *tnh* in Judg 5:11, 11:40; see Rabin, "The Emergence of Classical Hebrew," 71–71, 293 n. 4.

word occurs in Ps 68:23 where *bāšān* means "serpent" parallel to *yām*.[13]

This conclusion concerning the northern origin of the form *peten* is confirmed by the distribution of this word in the Bible. Four of the six usages of *peten* are in texts which evince non-Judahite origin: Deut 32:33, Job 20:14, 20:16, and our passage here in Ps 58:5. Only Isa 11:8 and Ps 91:13 appear in Judahite compositions. Presumably, the form *bāšān* became obsolete in Judahite Hebrew and the form *peten* then penetrated southward.[14]

6. The form *yahălōk* "he goes" in v. 9 retains the initial root letter *he* contrary to the norms of BH grammar. Such is also the case in Jer 9:3, Ps 91:6, Job 14:20, 16:6, 20:25. In addition, the 1csg imperfect *ʾehĕlōk* appears in Job 16:22, 23:8; the infinitive construct *(la)hălōk* occurs in Exod 3:19, Numb 22:13, 22:14, Job 34:23, Qoh 6:8; and plural imperative *hilĕkû* is used in Jer 51:50. The great majority of these attestations occur in non-Judahite environments. The two examples in Numbers 22 place us in the Balaam story, the six usages in Job place us in Transjordan as well, Qoh 6:8 occurs in a book with many northern affinities, and Jer 51:50 is an example of style-switching since this passage appears in the famous speech to Babylon. (Thus only Exod 3:19, Jer 9:3, Ps 91:6 are in texts without non-Judahite connections.)

The cognate evidence supports our conclusion. The imperfect *ʾhlk* appears in Moabite in Mesha Stele lines 14–15, and the form *hlk* may be the fsg imperative in Phoenician in Arslan Tash 1:21.[15] In other words, in other Canaanite dialects, the *he* was retained in parts of the verb where in BH it was typically elided. In light of the Moabite usage, special attention should be paid to the two occurrences in Numbers 22, one of which is in the mouth of the Moabites and one of which is in Balaam's speaking to the Moabites.

7. In v. 9 we also encounter *ʾēšet* "woman" in the absolute state.[16] The only other place in the Bible where this usage may possibly be

---

[13] Albright, "Catalogue of Early Hebrew Lyric Poems," 27; and Dahood, *Psalms II*, 145.

[14] It is not unusual in languages for such phenomena to occur via what linguists call dialect mixture. Thus Hebrew has doublets such as *nṣr* and *nṭr*, both meaning "guard," from a proto-Semitic root *nẓr*; English has doublets such as "shirt" and "skirt," "ship" and "skiff"; etc. See E. H. Sturtevant, *An Introduction to Linguistic Science* (New Haven: Yale University Press, 1947) 82–83.

[15] For discussion see Garr, *Dialect Geography*, 144–45.

[16] Needless to say, I hardly accept the view of Kraus, *Psalmen*, 1. 415: "Der stat. cstr. ist hier unmöglich und wird eine Verschreibung für *ʾiššāh* darstellen." Simi-

found is Prov 9:13.[17] If this is another example of absolute *ʾēšet*, then this attestation would similarly be in a northern composition. We have commented on a number of occasions on the northern affinities of Proverbs, especially the first nine chapters. In any case, absolute *ʾēšet* shows the retention of the final *-t*, which we have already noted is typical of Phoenician and IH (see above I.4).[18] The very word *ʾšt* is used in the absolute state in Phoenician in Karatepe inscription A, col. II, line 5.

8.   Also appearing in v. 9 is the negative particle *bal*. This too is a northern trait (see above I.5).

9.   In v. 11 the word *paʿam* is used for "foot." This usage is rare in Hebrew. However, since the cognates *pʿm* and *pʿn* are the regular words for "foot" in Phoenician and Ugaritic respectively[19] (the word *rgl* does not occur in these two languages), I would claim that *paʿam* = "foot" in Ps 58:11 is another marker of northern dialect. Indeed Ginsberg has already suggested that *paʿam* is a lexical feature distinguishing his Phoenic group from his Hebraic group.[20]

The other attestations of *paʿam* = "foot" in the Bible confirm this conclusion: Song 7:2, Ps 140:5, Isa 26:6, 2 Kgs 19:24 = Isa 37:25.[21] The first of these occurs in a book with northern affinities. The second of these appears in a poem with other IH characteristics (see below XIV.1). The last of these references occurs in Isaiah's speech placed in the mouth of Sennacherib, so I would explain this passage as another instance of style-switching. Mesopotamian invaders were consistently depicted in the Bible as coming from the north (Isa 14:31,

---

larly, there is no need to emend the word to *ʾāšût* "mole" as several scholars have suggested; see most recently K. Seybold, "Psalm lviii. Ein Lösungsversuch," *VT* 30 (1980) 59–60.

[17] Thus R. B. Y. Scott, *Proverbs-Ecclesiastes* (AB 18; Garden City, NY: Doubleday, 1965) 75; and Dahood, *Psalms II*, 62. Other passages suggested by scholars, such as Deut 21:11 and 1 Sam 28:7 (thus BDB, 61; KB, 92), may be otherwise explained (see GKC, 422).

[18] Technically, even in the absolute state there would be no reason not to expect *ʾēšet*. After all, it is only *-at* which shifts to *-āh*. A formation such as *ʾēšet* would not be effected. However, in the sense that Ps 58:9 has *ʾšt* instead of expected *ʾšh* (I dispense with the vowels for the present), the form may be considered a northern element.

[19] Tomback, *Phoenician and Punic*, 269; and Gordon, *Ugaritic Textbook*, 469.

[20] Ginsberg, "The Northwest Semitic Languages," 105.

[21] I do not include instances where *paʿam* is used for "footstep," e.g., Ps 17:5. Rather, I only have in mind instances where *paʿam* appears for an expected *regel*.

Jer 1:13, 6:22, Ezek 1:4, 26:7, etc.). Moreover, the present context portrays Sennacherib boasting about his conquest of Lebanon and its mountains and cedars (2 Kgs 19:23 = Isa 37:24). Thus it would not be surprising to have Isaiah portray the Assyrian king with a non-Judahite dialect.

This leaves only Isa 26:6 to explain. Here one has to admit that this attestation of *pa'am* is in a Judahite context. However, we may note that it is parallel to *regel* in this poetic passage, so that perhaps the poet had no choice but to use *pa'am* as the B word for the A word *regel*. In any case, the balance of the overall argument tips the scales in favor of the position that the use of *pa'am* = "foot" in the Bible is an indication of northern origin. This is especially the case in Ps 58:11,[22] occurring in a chapter with eight other elements of IH.

Summary

Nine linguistic features in Psalm 58 have northern affinities, thus pointing to the Israelian origin of the poem. An additional piece of evidence appears in the psalm, which may also favor this conclusion. I refer to the concluding phrase in v. 12: *ʾak yēš ʾĕlôhîm šôpĕṭîm bāʾāreṣ* "yea, there are gods who judge on the earth." The use of the plural participle *šôpĕṭîm*, which leads to the interpretation of *ʾĕlôhîm* as "gods" and not "God," would be more likely to arise in northern Israel. Judah was far from pristine, but the general impression one gets from biblical literature is that polytheistic syncretism was more common in the north.

---

[22] In addition, contrast the wording of this passage with *pa'am* to the wording of Ps 68:24 with *regel*. See Barr, *Comparative Philology and the Text of the Old Testament*, 192.

CHAPTER IX

Psalm 74

1. The relative pronoun *zeh* appears in v. 2.[1] As was argued above (I.2), the presence of this form in a section with other indications of IH may be used to bolster the claim for northern provenance.

2. Unquestionably v. 5 is one of the most difficult passages in the Bible.[2] The verb *yiwwāda'* causes most of the difficulty because it does not appear to be related to the usual meanings of the common root *yd'* "know." The only parallel in the entire Bible to this usage is Judg 8:16 *wayyōda'*, predicated of Gideon.[3] In both instances the context calls for "smite" as the basic meaning of the verb. Admittedly there are no Semitic cognates to put forward to justify this interpretation. But from this distribution of *yd'* = "smite" in the Bible (Psalm 74 and Gideon story), it is apparent that the verb was a feature of IH.

3. The noun *qardum-* "axe" in v. 5 is limited to non-Judahite texts in the Bible and its only cognate appears in Ugaritic. In the Bible it appears in 1 Sam 13:20–21 (reign of Saul), Judg 9:48 (story of Abimelech), and Jer 46:22 (in the prophet's address to Egypt[4]). In Ugaritic

---

[1] Briggs, *Psalms*, 2.157; and Dahood, *Psalms II*, 200–1.

[2] For a thorough review see J. A. Emerton, "Notes on Three Passages in Psalms Book III," *JTS* 14 (1963) 374–77. Needless to say, I reject the wholesale emendations introduced at the end of the verse by A. Robinson, "A Possible Solution to the Problem of Psalm 74:5," *ZAW* 89 (1977) 120–21.

[3] This was pointed out by N. Liebschutz, "An Interpretation of Psalm 74," *AJSL* 40 (1924) 285; and by J. P. Hyatt, "A Note on *yiwwāda'* in Ps. 74:5," *AJSL* 58 (1941) 99–100. The former emended the vowels of Ps 74:5 to conform to those of Judg 8:16. The latter accepted MT without alteration.

[4] For northern or Phoenician dialect in the prophets' speeches to Egypt, see above II.2.

it appears in Baal's epithet *aliy qrdm*.[5] We conclude, therefore, that this vocable was characteristic of IH, but that it was not used in JH.

4. The *hapax legomenon kaššîl* "hatchet" in v. 6 is known from Aramaic,[6] so that some scholars have labeled this noun an Aramaism.[7] Once more, however, it is better to view this word as a lexical item which was shared by IH and Aramaic, but which was not part of the JH vocabulary. For similar explanations see above II.5, V.2, VI.11, VI.15.

5. The verb *hlm* "strike" in v. 6 appears elsewhere in the Bible only in northern contexts and the only cognates in Semitic are Ugaritic and Phoenician *hlm*.[8] The other biblical attestations are Judg 5:22, 5:26 (in the Song of Deborah), Isa 16:8 (in the address to Moab), Isa 28:1 (in the address to Ephraim), Prov 23:35 (in a chapter with a particularly high concentration of northernisms[9]), and Ps 141:5 (see below XV.6). The one remaining occurrence is Isa 41:7; this Exilic usage will be explained according to the theory of the reunion of northern and southern Israelites in Babylonia. Furthermore, two nouns derived from the root *hlm* also occur only in northern texts. They are *halmût* "hammer" in Judg 5:26 and *mahălummôt* "blows" in Prov 18:6, 19:29.

6. In v. 13 *rā'šê tannînîm* "heads of the sea monsters" we encounter a double plural construction. This phraseology is to be contrasted with the similar example in Ezek 1:22 *rā'šê hahayyāh*, where the *nomen rectum* appears in the singular as expected. As discussed above (III.2) this syntagma is evidence of northern composition.

7. Almost a century ago J. Parisot opined that *nahărôt 'êtān* in v. 15 refers to the Jordan River at its strength.[10] This is not a piece of linguistic evidence, but it places us in a northern setting.

---

[5] See F. Willesen, "The Cultic Situation of Psalm lxxiv," *VT* 2 (1952) 304; Gordon, *Ugaritic Textbook*, 480; and Dahood, *Psalms II*, 202.

[6] Jastrow, *Dictionary*, 1.675–76. See also H. R. (C.) Cohen, *Biblical Hapax Legomena in the Light of Akkadian and Ugaritic* (SBLDS 37; Missoula, MT: Scholars Press, 1978) 96–97 n. 272.

[7] Briggs, *Psalms*, 2.158; and Wagner, *Aramaismen*, 68.

[8] Gordon, *Ugaritic Textbook*, 390; and Tomback, *Phoenician and Punic*, 81.

[9] Rendsburg, "Northern Origin," 117.

[10] J. Parisot, "Psaumes de la captivité," *RB* 4 (1895) 573, 576. However, this analysis is not entertained in the otherwise comprehensive treatment of J. A. Emerton, "'Spring and Torrent' in Psalm lxxiv 15," in *Volume du Congrès: Genève 1965* (SVT 15; Leiden: E. J. Brill, 1966) 122–33.

8. The first attestation of *ḥayyat* "beast"[11] in v. 19 is best understood as a feminine absolute noun ending in *-āt/-at*,[12] explained above (I.4) as an IH feature. Our standard texts contain the reading *ḥayyat*, while seventeen De Rossi codices vocalize *ḥayyāt*.[13]

Summary

Psalm 74 contains seven grammatical and lexical features of IH, and one passage suggests northern topography. Furthermore, it is part of the Asaph collection, wherein previous scholars have detected northern influences (see above, p. 14). Below (X) we shall see that the other poems in this group also reflect northern dialect. In addition, scholars have noted a number of thematic parallels between Psalm 74 and the Ugaritic texts.[14] All of this demonstrates that Psalm 74 must have originated in northern Israel. The reference to Zion in v. 2 is to be explained along the lines noted for Psalms 9–10. Obviously, there were Israelians who accepted the Zion theology dominant in Judah.

---

[11] Note the manner in which the poet is thus able to elicit the wordplay with *ḥayyat* "life of" in the second stich of the verse.

[12] Dahood, *Psalms II*, 207.

[13] This point is made by Briggs, *Psalms*, 2.160, and by J. Reider, "Contributions to the Hebrew Lexicon," *ZAW* 53 (1935) 271 n. 4. The De Rossi pointing cautions us against the conjectural emendations of some scholars.

[14] See most importantly Willesen, "The Cultic Situation of Psalm lxxiv," 289–306; and T. L. Fenton, "Gishot Shonot shel Sifre ha-Miqra' le-Mitos ha-Te'omakiya," in *Studies in Bible and the Ancient Near East Presented to Samuel E. Loewenstamm* (eds. Y. Avishur and J. Blau; Jerusalem: E. Rubinstein, 1978) 337–81. On vv. 13–14, see H. Donner, "Ugaritismen in der Psalmenforschung," *ZAW* 79 (1967) 338–44.

CHAPTER X

The Asaph Psalms

The northern provenance of selected psalms within the Asaph collection, chapters 50, 73–83, has been claimed by various scholars (see above, p. 14). Buss argued for a northern setting for the entire group.[1] Recently, Nasuti's monograph has discussed the origin of these psalms within the "Ephraimite tradition stream," and it has argued for treating these poems as an integrated unit (should this be a point of contention).[2] With the exception of Psalm 74 (see above IX), no single chapter within the Asaph group contains a large concentration of IH elements. But the collection as a whole does reflect northern dialect to a sufficient degree.

1. The first clue to the northern provenance of the Asaph psalms is the repeated mention of Joseph (77:16, 78:67, 80:2, 81:6) and Ephraim (78:9, 78:67, 80:3).[3] In addition, Benjamin and Manasseh are each mentioned once (80:13),[4] and victories over enemies from northern Israel's early history are recalled: Sisera and Jabin (83:10) and Oreb, Zeeb, Zebah, and Zalmunna (83:11).

Northern topography is not as present in the Asaph psalms as it is in the Korah psalms (see above VI.1), but it is likely that *harărê 'ēl*

---

[1] Buss, "The Psalms of Asaph and Korah."

[2] Nasuti, *Psalms of Asaph.*

[3] However, see also J. Hofbauer, "Psalm 77/78, ein 'politisch Lied'," *ZKT* 89 (1967) 41–50.

[4] The mention of Benjamin in Psalm 80 has puzzled interpreters of this chapter. If, as has been suggested often, the poem originates in the northern kingdom, why is Benjamin recalled? The answer is that of H. Heinemann ("The Date of Psalm 80," *JQR* 40 [1949–50] 297–302), that the psalm dates to the days of Saul. See also A. Roifer (Rofé), "Siyyumo shel Tehillim Pereq 80," *Tarbiz* 29 (1959–60) 124. But as we have mentioned at the outset (see above, p. 4, n. 18), material from the reign of Saul in 1 Samuel is also influenced by IH.

in Ps 50:10 (see below X.2) refers to the Lebanon range (see the opinion of Tournay cited above IV.3); that *nahărôt ʾêtān* in Ps 74:15 refers to the Jordan River at its strength (see above IX.7); and that *ʾarzê ʾēl* in Ps 80:11 refers to the cedars of Lebanon.

Two northern cities are mentioned in Ps 83:11, namely En-dor and Adamah (= Adam).[5] Furthermore, although the list of enemies in Ps 83:7–9 includes enemies on all sides of Israel, two specific peoples mentioned there were a concern only of the northern portion of the country. They are the Hagrites (v. 7), who are mentioned elsewhere in 1 Chr 5:10, 5:19–20 as opponents in Gilead,[6] and Ashur (v. 9), to be identified with the people mentioned in 2 Sam 2:9.[7]

2.   Of all the proposed instances of the conjunction *p* in the Bible (see above VI.10), the surest case is Ps 50:10, where *harĕrê ʾālep* is to be read as *harĕrê ʾēl* with the letter *pe* attached to the next verse.[8] The expression *harĕrê ʾālep*, whether translated as "mountains of thousand" or "mountains of oxen," is senseless.[9] Moreover, it is "syntactically impossible. The bound form before a numeral is unparalleled."[10] On the other hand, the phrase *harĕrê ʾēl* appears in Ps 36:7.[11]

---

[5]   For understanding *ʾădāmāh* as a toponym, see the brilliant article by E. Y. Kutscher, *"nišmĕdû bĕʿên dōʾr, hāyû dōmen lāʾădāmāh* (Tehillim 83,11)," *Yediʿot ha-Ḥevra ha-ʿIvrit le-Ḥaqirat ʾEreṣ Yiśraʾel ve-ʿAtiqoteha* 2 (1934–35) 40–42 (reprinted in Kutscher, *Hebrew and Aramaic Studies*, *šyṭ-škʾ*).

[6]   See Nasuti, *Psalms of Asaph*, 113 n. 266.

[7]   M. Lahav, "Mihu *hāʾăšûrî* (Shemuʾel Bet 2,9) ve-*ʾaššûr* (Tehillim 83,9)," *Beth Miqra* 28 (1983) 111–12. Although H. M. Wiener ("The Historical Background of Psalm lxxxiii," *JPOS* 8 [1928] 180–86) equated *ʾaššûr* with Assyria, he nonetheless realized that Psalm 83 is largely concerned with affairs of northern Israel.

[8]   M. Dahood, "Some Northwest-Semitic Words in Job," *Biblica* 38 (1957) 312; M. Dahood, *Ugaritic-Hebrew Philology* (Rome: Pontifical Biblical Institute, 1965) 35; and Dahood, *Psalms I*, 307–8. For an extremely detailed treatment of this verse, albeit with an opposite conclusion, see K. Aartun, "Textüberlieferung und vermeintliche Belege der Konjunktion *pV* im Alten Testament," *UF* 10 (1978) 5–7.

[9]   See the weak attempts to make some sense of *harĕrê ʾālep* by M. Mannati, "Le psaume 50 est-il un *rib*?" *Semitica* 23 (1973) 27–28; and H. Gese, "Psalm 50 und das alttestamentliche Gesetzesverständnis," in *Rechtfertigung: Festschrift für Ernst Käsemann zum 70. Geburtstag* (eds. J. Friedrich, W. Pohlmann, and P. Stuhlmacher; Tübingen: J. C. B. Mohr, 1976) 59–60.

[10]   Robertson, *Linguistic Evidence*, 133.

[11]   Numerous scholars, recognizing this fact, simply emend MT by dropping the *pe*. See Kraus, *Psalmen*, 1.371; and for a survey of opinions see Briggs, *Psalms*, 1.421.

3. Reduplicatory plural forms (see above IV.3) appear three times in the Asaph psalms: *harĕrê* "mountains of" in Ps 50:10, 76:5, and *ḥăṣāṣekâ* "your arrows" in 77:18.

4. The consonant *yod* is retained in the inflection of III*y* verbs in four instances (see above IV.4). They are Ps 73:2Q *nāṭāyû* "turned aside,"[12] Ps 77:4 *ʾehĕmāyāh* "moan," Ps 78:44 *yištāyûn* "drink," and Ps 83:3 *yehĕmāyûn* "moan."

5. The *hapax legomenon* *ʾûl* "strength, body" in Ps 73:4 was first associated with Ugaritic *ul* (*UT* Krt:88) by Ginsberg,[13] and this identification has been accepted by numerous scholars.[14] This vocable must have been at home in northern dialects, and apparently it did not penetrate southward to Judah.

6. The *hapax legomenon* *yāmîqû* "they mock" in Ps 73:8, from the root *mwq*, "is well attested in various dialects of Aramaic."[15] Briggs, Podechard, Kautzsch, and Wagner all considered it to be an Aramaism.[16] As we have seen on several occasions above (II.5, V.2, VI.11, VI.15, IX.4), instead of simply labeling such a word an Aramaism, it is better to adjust this view slightly and to posit that *mwq* represents a shared lexical feature between Aramaic and IH.

7. The *hapax legomenon* *ʾeštônān* in Ps 73:21 is generally derived from the Hebrew verb *šnn* "sharpen."[17] An apparently related form *yšnn* appears in Ugaritic in *UT* 125:12, and this verb is usually taken to mean "gnash one's teeth" as a denominative from *šn* "tooth."[18] As

---

[12] For discussion see A. Caquot, "Le psaume lxxiii," *Semitica* 21 (1971) 34–35; J. F. Ross, "Psalm 73," in *Israelite Wisdom: Theological and Literary Essays in Honor of Samuel Terrien* (eds. J. G. Gammie, W. A. Brueggemann, W. L. Humphreys, and J. M. Ward; New York: Union Theological Seminary, 1978) 170 n. 8; and H. Irsigler, *Psalm 73—Monolog eines Weisen* (St. Ottilien: EOS Verlag, 1984) 11–13.

[13] H. L. Ginsberg, *The Legend of King Keret* (BASORSS 2–3; New Haven: American Schools of Oriental Research, 1946) 37.

[14] Dahood, *Psalms II,* 189; Caquot, "Le psaume lxxiii," 36; Ross, "Psalm 73," 171 n. 13; and Irsigler, *Psalm 73,* 16–17.

[15] Greenspahn, *Hapax Legomena in Biblical Hebrew,* 133.

[16] Briggs, *Psalms,* 2.148; E. Podechard, "Notes sur les psaumes," *RB* 32 (1923) 243; Kautzsch, *Aramaismen,* 53; and Wagner, *Aramaismen,* 73. See also Caquot, "Le psaume lxxiii," 38–39; and Irsigler, *Psalm 73,* 20.

[17] BDB, 1041–42; and KB, 998.

[18] Gordon, *Ugaritic Textbook,* 493; and J. Gray, *The Krt Text in the Literature of Ras Shamra* (Leiden: E. J. Brill, 1964) 66.

Avishur has shown, in neither case can these translations be substantiated. Instead, in both contexts the meaning "cry, weep, lament" is more appropriate, and indeed medieval Hebrew poets understood the word thus.[19] Accordingly, it is more than probable that we should recognize in *šnn* "cry, weep, lament" a northern Canaanite vocable attested in Ugaritic and IH.

8.   Twice in the Asaph collection, in Ps 73:22 and Ps 76:11, we encounter the fsg nominal ending *-ôt* (see above II.6). From the context of Ps 73:22 it is clear that *běhēmôt* is singular, and this is how the ancient versions understood the form.[20] Accordingly, Dahood is correct in positing the northern fsg nominal ending *-ôt* here.[21]

The apparently plural form *hēmōt* in Ps 76:11 appears elsewhere only in Prov 22:24. In both of these attestations, it is best to assume that the form is singular, to be translated simply "wrath."[22] This is the understanding of both the Septuagint and the Vulgate at Ps 76:11.[23]

9.   The noun *hāmar* "wine" in Ps 75:9 occurs in slightly different form in Deut 32:14 *hāmer* (pausal), Isa 27:2 *hemer*.[24] This distribution suggests a northern home for this vocable. The Israelian origin of Deuteronomy 32 has been noted above (p. 12), and if Isaiah 24–27 is Exilic or post-Exilic then the use of *hemer* here is explained through the reunion of northern and southern exiles.

The cognates to Hebrew *hmr* (I dispense with the vowels for the moment) are all to be found in languages spoken to the north and east of Israel: Aramaic, Phoenician, Ugaritic, and Deir ꜥAlla.[25] The

---

[19] Y. Avishur, "*Wěkilyôtay ꜂eštônān* (Tehillim 73:21)," *Leshonenu* 44 (1979–80) 263–67; and Avishur, *Stylistic Studies of Word-Pairs*, 723–25.

[20] See Caquot, "Le psaume lxxiii," 50. For a survey of opinions on this form see Irsigler, *Psalm 73*, 40–41.

[21] Dahood, *Psalms II*, 194.

[22] For complete analysis of the verse, including a survey of opinions concerning *hēmōt*, see J. A. Emerton, "A Neglected Solution of a Problem in Psalm lxxvi 11," *VT* 24 (1974) 136–46. See also J. Day, "Shear-Jashub (Isaiah vii 3) and 'The Remnant of Wrath' (Psalm lxxvi 11)," *VT* 31 (1981) 77. A thorough investigation of this verse also appears in O. Eissfeldt, "Psalm 76," *TLZ* 82 (1957) 801–8 (reprinted in Eissfeldt, *Kleine Schriften*, 3.448–57), though the wholesale emendations introduced by Eissfeldt lessen the value of this article for our present purposes.

[23] Briggs, *Psalms*, 2.170.

[24] See the brief comments of R. Tournay, "Notes sur les psaumes," *RB* 79 (1972) 47–48.

[25] For Aramaic see Jastrow, *Dictionary*, 1.480; BDB, 1093; and KB, 1076. For Phoenician see Tomback, *Phoenician and Punic*, 107. For Ugaritic see Gordon,

Deir ʿAlla usage and the two Phoenician attestations of *ḥmr*, which come from Shiqmona, place this root within or exceedingly close to the boundaries of the northern kingdom of Israel. Although cognates to JH *yayin* "wine" appear in Ugaritic[26] and in IH,[27] note that the form does not occur in Aramaic, Phoenician, and Deir ʿAlla. Based on the distribution of the biblical examples, the extra-biblical evidence, and the linguistic opposition, there can be little doubt that *ḥmr* was a feature of northern dialectal Hebrew.

10. Also appearing in Ps 75:9 is the *hapax legomenon mesek* "mixed wine." This form has its sole Semitic cognate in Ugaritic *msk*.[28] A very similar noun *mimsāk* "mixed wine" occurs in Isa 65:11, Prov 23:30. The latter passage places us once more in one of the most Phoenicianizing of all chapters in Proverbs (see above IX.5). The former passage, written during the Exile, presumably used this word upon the reunion of the exiles in Mesopotamia. Furthermore, note that "mixed drinks are attributed to a foreign cult" in this verse.[29]

Another similar noun is *māzeg* (pausal) "mixed wine" in Song 7:3. This form contains the consonants of the Aramaic form *mzg*, and should also enter into our discussion.[30] Wagner considered *māzeg* in Song 7:3 an Aramaism,[31] but again it is more accurate to speak of the form as a lexeme shared by Aramaic and IH.

A verb *msk* "mix" also exists in BH, and its distribution points to a northern home. Two of the attestations, Prov 9:2, 9:5, are in a section of Proverbs replete with IH features (see above, p. 10). Isa 19:14 occurs in the oracle against Egypt, so a Phoenicianism is not unexpected here (see above p. 31, n. 10). Ps 102:10 occurs in an Exilic poem, so the theory of the reunion of the exiles can be advanced to explain this usage, and we may also point out that a thematic parallel with UT 62:10 is present.[32] Thus only Isa 5:22 is in a decidedly Judahite con-

---

Ugaritic Textbook, 402. For Deir ʿAlla see Hackett, *The Balaam Text from Deir ʿAllā*, 129. The root is also to be found in South Semitic (Arabic and South Arabian).

[26] Gordon, *Ugaritic Textbook*, 410.

[27] In the Samaria ostraca.

[28] Gordon, *Ugaritic Textbook*, 435.

[29] J. P. Brown, "The Mediterranean Vocabulary of the Vine," *VT* 19 (1969) 153.

[30] See Brown, "The Mediterranean Vocabulary of the Vine," 153–55; Tournay, "Notes sur les psaumes," 48; and Pope, *Song of Songs*, 619–20. All of these scholars correlate the Indo-European evidence (specifically Greek, Latin, and Sanskrit) as well.

[31] Wagner, *Aramaismen*, 73–74. See also M. V. Fox, *The Song of Songs and the Ancient Egyptian Love Songs* (Madison: University of Wisconsin, 1985) 189.

[32] Brown, "The Mediterranean Vocabulary of the Vine," 155.

text. However, note that here *msk* is used as the B-word in parallelism with *šth* "drink."

All of this evidence converges to demonstrate that *mesek* "mixed wine" in Ps 75:9 should be considered an IH element.

11. The form *ʾeštôlĕlû* in Ps 76:6, regardless of its meaning,[33] is best understood as a Hebrew parallel to the Aramaic *ʾetpaʿʿal* with IIgem verb. Briggs and Wagner labeled this usage an Aramaism.[34] However, it is more accurate to posit that in areas of northern Israel the *ʾt-* prefix was used instead of the *ht-* prefix for the T-stem verb.

12. Double plural constructions occur in Ps 77:6 *šĕnôt ʿôlāmîm* "years of eternities," and Ps 78:49 *malʾăkê rāʿîm* "messengers of evils." The latter phrase should be contrasted with the similar examples in Isa 14:32, 33:7, where the standard usage of a singular *nomen rectum* appears. This syntagma is a characteristic of IH (see above III.2).

13. The plural form *miškĕnôt* in Ps 78:28 with singular connotation "tabernacle" was identified above (VI.3) as a feature of IH.

14. The verb *hitwû* (H-stem of *twh*) in Ps 78:41 is a *hapax legomenon* meaning "grieved."[35] The sole cognates to this word are in Syriac and Aramaic meaning "be regretful, be disgusted, etc."[36] Accordingly, we have another example of a lexeme whose home bridged the Aramean and Israelian territories (see above II.5, V.2, VI.11, VI.15, IX.4, X.6).

15. The form *bal* in Ps 78:44 has been identified above (I.5) as a feature of IH.

16. The verbal root *pls* "weigh, make level, straighten" in Ps 78:50 has been identified above (VIII.3) as a northern characteristic.

---

[33] For brief discussion see F. Zorell, "Zu Ps 12,9; 76,6," *Biblica* 10 (1929) 100.

[34] Briggs, *Psalms*, 2.165, 169; and Wagner, *Aramaismen*, 137.

[35] The forms in 1 Sam 21:14, Ezek 9:4, are from a different root *twh* meaning "make a mark," denominative from *taw* "mark."

[36] J. Payne Smith, *A Compendious Syriac Dictionary* (Oxford: Clarendon, 1903) 605–6; and Jastrow, *Dictionary*, 2.1651. See also Emerton, "Notes on Three Passages in Psalms Book III," 381.

17. The relative pronoun *zeh* appears in Ps 78:54.[37] As noted above (I.2), the presence of this form in a section with other indications of IH adds support to the claim for northern provenance.

18. The form *kannāh* in Ps 80:16 has engendered much discussion.[38] The proper solution is that which scholars often mention, but then express doubts about,[39] namely, that *kannāh* equals Syriac *kana?* "stem, stalk, root."[40] This meaning fits the context of vv. 9–17, with the metaphorical usage of the planting of the vine. Thus we have yet another example of a vocable shared by Aramaic (Syriac) and IH (see above II.5, V.2, VI.11, VI.15, IX.4, X.6, X.14).

19. The verbal root *ksh* "cut down"[41] in Ps 80:17 appears again only in Isa 33:12. Since the root is relatively common in Aramaic,[42] there is reason to assume that it may have been a feature of IH as well.[43] This is borne out by the distribution of this verb in the Bible. Ps 80:17 occurs in the Asaph psalms with numerous other IH characteristics, and Isa 33:12 is in the prophet's address to Assyria. Since we know that the Assyrians used Aramaic widely during the 8th Century, it is likely that Isaiah has peppered his address with Aramaic forms in a variation of style-switching.

20. The noun *keseh* "full moon" in Ps 81:4 is an obvious northernism. It appears again only in Prov 7:20, where it is spelled *kese?*,[44] in a section of Proverbs laden with IH elements. Cognates occur in the languages used to the north of Israel, namely, Phoenician and Ugaritic.[45]

---

[37] Briggs, *Psalms*, 2.196; and Dahood, *Psalms II*, 245.

[38] See, e.g., F. Zorell, "Psalm 80. Gebet für das Volk Gottes," *BZ* 15 (1921) 124; and G. Rinaldi, "Nota," *Bibbia e Oriente* 22 (1980) 124.

[39] See, e.g., BDB, 488; and D. Hill, "'Son of Man' in Psalm 80 v. 17," *NT* 15 (1973) 263 n. 1.

[40] Payne Smith, *A Compendious Syriac Dictionary*, 217: "*the stem* of a tree, *stalk*, *root* of a plant."

[41] There have been attempts to treat *kĕsûḥāh* as the preposition *ke-* and the noun *sûḥāh*. But the verb *ksh* is to be retained here; see Roifer (Rofé), "Siyyumo shel Tehillim Pereq 80," 120 n. 26.

[42] Jastrow, *Dictionary*, 1.652–53.

[43] Typically, Briggs (*Psalms*, 2.203, 209) considered the word an Aramaism.

[44] For general discussion of the term see S. B. Freehof, "Sound the Shofar—'Ba-Kesse' Psalm 81:4," *JQR* 64 (1973–74) 225–28.

[45] For Phoenician see Tomback, *Phoenician and Punic*, 146. For Ugaritic see the documentation given by M. Dahood, "Hebrew-Ugaritic Lexicography III," *Biblica* 46 (1965) 330; and Dahood, *Psalms II*, 264.

21. The word *nāʿîm* "pleasant" in Ps 81:3 derives from the root *nʿm*. The northern distribution of this vocable has been discussed above (II.4).

22. The form *bîhôsēp* "in Joseph" in Ps 81:6 retains the *he* in a proper name which morphologically is a Hiphʿil imperfect. This usage has been identified above (V.8) as a feature of IH.

23. In Ps 81:17 *ḥēleb* is parallel to *ṣûr*. Since the latter means "rock," it is very doubtful if the former is to be assigned its usual meaning of "fat" in this passage. Rather, as Kutscher proposed,[46] *ḥēleb* means "hill" here, to be equated with the exceedingly common Ugaritic word *ḥlb*.[47] The rareness of this word in BH is no doubt attributable to its having been limited geographically to the northern extremes of ancient Israel.[48]

Summary

This array of linguistic evidence proves the essential correctness of Buss' view that the Asaph psalms originate in northern Israel. As noted earlier (p. 14), other scholars have concluded similarly for individual poems within the Asaph collection.[49] We should also note that still other scholars have noted important literary and thematic parallels between these poems and Ugaritic poetry.[50] Obviously, all

[46] E. Y. Kutscher, "Be-Shuley ha-Millon ha-Miqraʾi," *Leshonenu* 32 (1967–68) 346 (reprinted in Kutscher, *Hebrew and Aramaic Studies*, *šnḥ*). This interpretation has been accepted by Dahood, *Psalms II*, 267; and by Avishur, *Stylistic Studies of Word-Pairs*, 430.

[47] Gordon, *Ugaritic Textbook*, 402. Note that Ugaritic *ḥlb* is often parallel to *ǵr*, just as *ḥēleb* is parallel to *ṣûr* in Ps 80:17.

[48] One wonders if *ḥēleb* in Ps 73:7 is not also to be translated as "hill." Note the use of *gaʾăwāh* "haughtiness" in v. 6 and *mārôm* "heights" in v. 8. The verse is too difficult, however, to be assured of any conclusions. For discussion see Irsigler, *Psalm 73*, 17–20; and A. Roifer (Rofé), "*yāṣāʾ mēḥēleb ʿênēmô*," *Tarbiz* 32 (1962–63) 109–13.

[49] To the authors cited earlier, add Briggs, *Psalms*, 2.203 (on Psalm 80); B. Z. Dinaburg, "Pereq bi-Thillim mi-Zemano shel Hosheaʿ ben ʾElah," *Qoveṣ ha-Ḥevra ha-ʿIvrit le-Ḥaqirat ʾEreṣ Yiśraʾel ve-ʿAtiqoteha* (= *JJPES*) (1928) 250–61 (on Psalm 80); Dahood, *Psalms II*, 255, 263 (on Psalms 80 and 81); and A. Weiser, *The Psalms* (OTL; Philadelphia: Westminster, 1962) 553 (on Psalm 81).

[50] R. T. O'Callaghan, "A Note on the Canaanite Background of Psalm 82," *CBQ* 15 (1953) 311–14; H. Ringgren, "Einige Bemerkungen zum lxxiii. Psalm," *VT*

the Psalms share motifs with Ugaritic literature, but it does appear that the Asaph group has an even greater proportion of such nexuses. In a similar vein, Nasuti noted several striking parallels between the Asaph psalms and Deuteronomy 32, another northern composition.[51]

Furthermore, several studies have demonstrated that the history of Israel which is presented in the Asaph psalms is at times at variance with the canonical presentation in the Pentateuch. Here I would mention Loewenstamm's important article on Psalm 81[52] and A. F. Campbell's extended discussion of Psalm 78.[53] The reason behind such differences is that Israelian traditions appear in the Asaph psalms, and they are not necessarily the same as those which became standardized in the Pentateuch, an essentially Judahite composition.[54] In short, the evidence converges to defend the hypothesis of the northern provenance of Psalms 50, 73–83.

---

3 (1953) 265–72, especially pp. 267–69; H. G. Jefferson, "Psalm lxxvii," *VT* 13 (1963) 87–91; A. Gonzalez, "Le psaume lxxxii," *VT* 13 (1963) 293–309; M. Tsevat, "God and the Gods in Assembly," *HUCA* 40–41 (1969–70) 123–37 (reprinted in M. Tsevat, *The Meaning of the Book of Job and Other Studies* [New York: Ktav, 1980] 131–47); O. Loretz, "Psalmenstudien," *UF* 3 (1971) 113–15 (where Psalm 82 is referred to as "eine kanaanäische *short story*"); M. Mannati, "Les adorateurs de Mot dans le psaume lxxiii," *VT* 22 (1972) 420–25; S. Cavalletti, "Proposta di lettura del Sal. 78,65," *RBI* 26 (1978) 337–40; and S. Cavalletti, "Il dio ebbro di vino," *Ricerche Bibliche e Religiose* 15 (1981) 135–36.

51 See, e.g., Nasuti, *Psalms of Asaph*, 110, 114.

52 Loewenstamm, "ʿēdût bîhôsēp."

53 A. F. Campbell, "Psalm 78: A Contribution to the Theology of Tenth Century Israel," *CBQ* 41 (1979) 51–79, especially pp. 64–70. I disagree, however, with Campbell's ultimate conclusion; see the following note.

54 This was understood by Loewenstamm, but not by Campbell. Campbell ascribed the differences between Psalm 78 and the book of Exodus to the former's having been composed before the latter became the standard account in ancient Israel. But since we have demonstrated that Psalm 78 is northern, and since we can demonstrate that the Pentateuch is essentially southern, regional variation is the best explanation for such differences. Very briefly, I can illustrate the Judahite origin of the Pentateuch in the following manner. If we accept, for the moment, the existence of the J - E - D - P documents, it is obvious that J and P are ascribed by scholars to the south virtually without exception. As noted above (p. 12, n. 50), E and D are generally devoid of IH features as well. Consequently, except for a few texts such as Deuteronomy 32, the Pentateuch is on the whole a Judahite composition.

CHAPTER XI

Psalm 116

1. The form *yĕhôšîaᶜ* "he will save" in v. 6 is another example of the non-elision of *he* in Hiphᶜal/Hophᶜal imperfects and participles. Above (V.8) we adduced that this was a characteristic of IH.

2. Three times in this psalm we encounter the 2fsg pronominal suffix *-kî*, in contrast to the standard BH form *-k*. The three vocables are *mĕnûḥāyĕkî* "your rest" (v. 7), *ᶜālāyĕkî* "upon you" (v. 7), and *bĕtôkēkî* "in your midst" (v. 19). Scholars have been virtually unanimous in judging this form to be an Aramaism.[1] Obviously, the appearance of 2fsg *-kî* in various biblical texts is due to Aramaic influence. This will explain its presence in Jer 11:15, Ps 103:3 (bis), 103:4 (bis), 103:5, 135:9, 137:6, all dating to the period immediately before, during, or after the Exile.[2]

However, the five other occurrences of 2fsg *-kî* in the Bible are in 2 Kgs 4:2K, 4:3K, 4:7K (bis), Song 2:13K. These attestations suggest that this morpheme was an IH feature.[3] The first four passages are all in the mouth of Elisha. Not only is he a northern prophet, but in a previous study I was able to further localize his home to the territory of Gilead.[4] The fifth of these examples is from the Song of Songs, whose northern affinities has been mentioned above (p. 11). In light

---

[1] See Wagner, *Aramaismen*, 130, for discussion and bibliography.

[2] The date of Jeremiah is obvious. On the post-Exilic dating of Psalm 103 see the detailed discussion in Hurvitz, *Beyn Lashon le-Lashon*, 107–152. Almost all scholars would date Psalm 135 to the post-Exilic period. And the contents of Psalm 137 obviously point to its authorship during the Exile.

[3] This was already noted by Burney, *Kings*, 208. See also Rendsburg, "Morphological Evidence."

[4] G. A. Rendsburg, "A Reconstruction of Moabite-Israelite History," *JANES* 13 (1981) 67–73, especially p. 71.

of this latter set of attestations of -*kî*, I conclude that it was a feature of IH.

3. The phrase *ʾarṣôt haḥayyîm* "lands of the living" in v. 9 is another example of a double plural construction. Above (III.2) we concluded that this is an element of IH.

4. The phrase in v. 10 *heʾĕmantî kî ʾădabbēr* has traditionally been rendered something like "I trusted even when I spoke" (thus JPSV). This is an admittedly peculiar expression. A major step towards the proper elucidation of this passage was made by G. R. Driver, who suggested that *ʾădabbēr* derives not from *dbr* "speak," rather from a homonymous root *dbr* "carry off, pursue."[5] The desired Semitic cognate for this verb is Aramaic *dbr* with the same meaning. More and more scholars seem ready to accede to this opinion,[6] and I too am convinced. Accordingly, this lexeme represents another isogloss bridging Aramaic and IH (for others see above II.5, V.2, VI.11, VI.15, IX.4, X.6, X.14, X.18, X.19).

Now, this interpretation necessitates revocalizing the text to read a passive *ʾeddabbēr* (so Driver) or a Puʿal *ʾădubbār* (so Dahood), thus yielding the sense "I trusted even when I was pursued." This violates my own dictum of not tampering with MT, consonants and vowels alike. However, I believe that the entire three vv. 9–11 are to be understood as a Janus construction with our word *ʾdbr* as the pivot point.[7] Note that the verb in v. 9a is *ʾethallēk* signifying motion and the verb in v. 11a is *ʾāmartî* signifying speech. In between stands the root *dbr* in v. 10a, which at the same time implies both motion ("carry off, pursue") and speech ("speak"). Once the text was overlaid with vowels, a decision had to be made whether to point the word as a passive or an active. Obviously the choice was to vocalize *ʾdbr* as active *ʾădabbēr* looking ahead to *ʾāmartî* in the next verse. But the word still means "carried off, pursued" echoing *ʾethallēk* in the preceding verse.

---

[5] G. R. Driver, "Studies on the Vocabulary of the Old Testament. VII," *JTS* 35 (1934) 382. See also Barr, *Comparative Philology and the Text of the Old Testament*, 324.

[6] E.g., M. Dahood, *Psalms III* (Garden City, NY: Doubleday, 1970) 148.

[7] On this feature of biblical poetry, see C. H. Gordon, "New Directions," *BASP* 15 (Naphtali Lewis Festschrift) (1978) 59–60; G. A. Rendsburg, "Janus Parallelism in Gen 49:26," *JBL* 99 (1980) 291–93; E. Zurro, "Disemia de *brḥ* y paralelismo bifronte en Job 9,25," *Biblica* 62 (1981) 546–47; and W. G. E. Watson, *Classical Hebrew Poetry: A Guide to its Techniques* (JSOTSS 26; Sheffield: JSOT Press, 1984) 159.

5. In v. 12 appears the unique 3msg pronominal suffix *-ôhî* in the word *tagmûlôhî* "his good deeds." This usage is almost always characterized as an Aramaism,[8] but new evidence forces us to evaluate *-ôhî* afresh.[9] It is true that *-wh* is the Aramaic 3msg pronominal suffix attached to plural nouns,[10] but the same form is now attested at Deir ʿAlla.[11] In addition, Moabite *-h* probably was vocalized somewhat similarly.[12] Accordingly, 3msg *-ôhî* need not *a priori* be labeled an Aramaism. It clearly was at home in the Canaanite sphere, albeit not in Judah and thus not in standard BH. Instead, this morpheme should be considered an element of IH.[13]

6. The word *yāqār* in v. 15 has been the subject of much debate. The usual meanings of this word, "precious, costly, expensive," simply do not make sense within the context of the passage. Recently, J. A. Emerton advanced the discussion significantly with his suggestion that *yāqār* be understood as "grievous," which meaning this word has in Aramaic.[14] This opinion is certainly correct. Emerton also noted that an Aramaism such as *yāqār* = "grievous" is not unexpected in this psalm in light of the forms *tagmûlôhî*, *ʾālāyĕkî*, *bĕtôkĕkî* (he seems to have overlooked *mĕnûḥāyĕkî*).[15] I would slightly adjust this observation by claiming that this use of *yāqār* is not an Aramaism as most scholars understand this term, rather it is an element of IH. As such it

---

[8] Again see Wagner, *Aramaismen*, 130, for discussion and bibliography.

[9] See Rendsburg, "Morphological Evidence."

[10] Segert, *Altaramäische Grammatik*, 169–70; and R. Degen, *Altaramäische Grammatik* (Wiesbaden: Franz Steiner, 1969) 57.

[11] Hackett, *The Balaam Text from Deir ʿAllā*, 115–16; and Garr, *Dialect Geography*, 108.

[12] J. Naveh, "Review of J. Hoftijzer and G. van der Kooij, *Aramaic Texts from Deir ʿAlla*," *IEJ* 29 (1979) 136; J. C. Greenfield, "Review of J. Hoftijzer and G. van der Kooij, *Aramaic Texts from Deir ʿAlla*," *JSS* 25 (1980) 250; and Garr, *Dialect Geography*, 108.

[13] Hackett (*The Balaam Text from Deir ʿAllā*, 115–16) stated that *-wh* appears "in Aramaic and never in Canaanite" and that it does not occur "in previously known Canaanite texts." But this claim needs to be adjusted. It patently does occur in Ps 116:12. Ironically, Hackett referred to the presence of *-wh* in Deir ʿAlla as "the strongest argument for the Aramaic classification of the text." Had Hackett cited this unique occurrence in the Bible, she would have removed the sole nexus with Aramaic and further bolstered her argument that the language of the Deir ʿAlla texts is Canaanite.

[14] J. A. Emerton, "How Does the Lord Regard the Death of His Saints in Psalm cxvi 15?" *JTS* 84 (1983) 146–56.

[15] Ibid., 154.

represents still another instance of a lexical link between IH and Aramaic (see the list of examples above XI.4).

Summary

On the basis of these six grammatical usages, I conclude that Psalm 116 is another example of an Israelian composition. Moreover, in the present instance, we may even be able to further pinpoint the geographical origin of this psalm. Two of the features have clear Transjordanian parallels. The 2fsg pronominal suffix *-kî* is reflected in the Elisha story, and the 3msg pronominal suffix *-ôhî* occurs at Deir ʿAlla and probably in Moabite. If I may be so bold, I would suggest that Psalm 116 emanates from the territory of Gilead.

The linguistic approach to Psalm 116 also militates against the view that this chapter was originally two separate compositions, divided between vv. 1–9 and 10–19. This division is already visible in the LXX and some modern scholars have suggested the same. Similarly, other scholars have maintained that various verses scattered here and there in Psalm 116 are secondary.[16] However, in the above analysis we have isolated northern linguistic features in vv. 6, 7, 9, 10, 12, 15, and 19. Whatever theories have been advanced by scholars concerning the lack of unity in Psalm 116 are greatly weakened in the light of this distribution.

---

[16] For a discussion of the various views, see ibid., 147–48.

CHAPTER XII

Psalm 132

1. The divine epithet *ʾăbîr yaʿăqōb* occurs twice in this chapter, in vv. 2 and 5.[1] Elsewhere in the Bible it appears in Gen 49:24, Isa 49:26, 60:16. The first of these attestations is within Jacob's blessing to Joseph, thus suggesting a northern origin for the expression.[2] The two passages from Second Isaiah would be another example of IH elements reemerging in Exilic and post-Exilic texts after the reunion of northern and southern exiles in Mesopotamia.

2. In v. 4 *šěnat* "sleep" evinces the northern fsg nominal ending -*at* (see above I.4).

3. Twice in this psalm, in vv. 5 and 7 the form *miškěnôt*, morphologically plural, is used to mean "tabernacle" in the singular. Above (VI.3) we commented on this usage as a characteristic of IH.

4. In v. 6 we encounter the toponym *ʾeprātāh* parallel to *śědê yāʿar* "woodlands." Most scholars have interpreted these terms in light of the following: a) vv. 5–8 deal with the tabernacle and the ark, b) vv. 13–14 refer to Zion as their permanent home, and c) vv. 1, 10, 11, 17 refer to David, Accordingly, scholars have assumed that the entire poem deals with the transfer of Israel's shrine to Jerusalem as described in 2 Samuel 6. Thus, many conclude that *ʾeprātāh* refers to Bethlehem (based on Gen 35:19, Mic 5:1, Ruth 1:2, 4:11, etc.), that is,

---

[1] For complete discussion of this term see N. M. Sarna, "The Divine Title *ʾabîr yaʿăqôbh*," in *Essays on the Occasion of the Seventieth Anniversary of the Dropsie University* (eds. A. I. Katsh and L. Nemoy; Philadelphia: Dropsie University, 1979) 389–96.

[2] This has been suggested previously by J. Schreiner, *Sion-Jerusalem Jahwes Königssitz* (Munich: Kösel-Verlag, 1963) 177–78 n. 17.

the birthplace of David, and that *śĕdê yā'ar* is a poetic designation for Kirjath-jearim, where presumably the ark rested before its transfer to Jerusalem (see 1 Sam 7:1, 2 Sam 6:2).[3] However, the situation is not that simple. First of all, the ark has nothing to do with Bethlehem.[4] Secondly, *'eprāt(āh)* refers to more than one geographic locale in the Bible.[5] Third, it cannot be proved that *śĕdê yā'ar* designates Kirjath-jearim in Ps 132:6. Moreover, even if it did, a) this toponym also refers to more than one place in the Bible,[6] and b) it cannot be firmly established that the house of Abinadab where the ark rested for twenty years was in Kirjath-jearim.[7]

I prefer to interpret *'eprātāh* in v. 6 as an alternative designation for Ephraim.[8] The form *'eprātî* is the only gentilic of Ephraim which the Bible uses (Judg 12:5, 1 Sam 1:1, 1 Kgs 11:26). The term *'eprātāh* in Ps 132:6, then, would be a back formation from the gentilic. This connotation makes much more sense when we realize that the home of the ark for most of Israel's early history was in Shiloh in the territory of Ephraim. This, in turn, explains *śĕdê yā'ar*, for as I. Finkelstein has discussed recently, the territory of Ephraim included much of the forested areas of the central hill country.[9] Our ability to elucidate properly the terms in v. 6 adds weight to our argument that the psalm is an Israelian composition.[10]

5. In the phrase *qûmāh yhwh limnûḥātekâ* in v. 8, the *l* almost certainly means "from," so that these words are to be translated "arise, O

---

[3] See, e.g., Kraus, *Psalmen*, 2.885. For extended discussion see O. Eissfeldt, "Psalm 132," *WO* 2 (1954–59) 480–483, in particular p. 482 (reprinted in Eissfeldt, *Kleine Schriften*, 3.481–485, in particular p. 484).

[4] This objection was already raised by Buttenweiser, *Psalms*, 378.

[5] See M. D. Cassuto, "'Eprat, 'Epratah," *EM* 1 (1950) 515–16.

[6] B. Mazar, "Qiryat Ye'arim," *EM* 7 (1976) 270–72; and P. K. McCarter, *II Samuel* (AB 9; Garden City, NY: Doubleday, 1984) 176, with bibliography.

[7] This is not the proper place for extended discussion of this issue; see P. K. McCarter, *I Samuel* (AB 8; Garden City, NY: Doubleday, 1980) 137.

[8] Thus Weiser, *The Psalms*, 780; and Schreiner, *Sion-Jerusalem Jahwes Königssitz*, 49. This option has also been raised by T. E. Fretheim, "Psalm 132: A Form-Critical Study," *JBL* 86 (1967) 296–97; and A. Robinson, "Do Ephrathah and Jaar Really Appear in Psalm 132:6?" *ZAW* 86 (1974) 220.

[9] I. Finkelstein, *The Archaeology of the Israelite Settlement* (Jerusalem: Israel Exploration Society, 1988) 200.

[10] Is it only coincidence that the Targum to Psalms interprets *śĕdê yā'ar* as Lebanon? See further Briggs, *Psalms*, 2. 470; and Robinson, "Do Ephrathah and Jaar Really Appear in Psalm 132:6?" 221.

Yahweh, from your resting place."[11] This has already been identified
as a feature of IH (see above, I.3).

6. In v. 12 *ʿēdôtî* "my testimony" must be a feminine singular noun.
The 1csg pronominal suffix indicates this, otherwise the ending
would be *-ay*.[12] For additional examples of fsg *-ôt* in Israelian texts see
above II.6, V.1, VII.1, VIII.1, X.8.

7. The received texts points consonantal *zw* in v. 12 as the fsg
demonstrative pronoun *zô*. If this interpretation is correct, then we
have another IH feature in this poem. Elsewhere this form occurs in
Hos 7:16, that is, in a northern prophet; and spelled *zōh* it appears in
the mouth of Elisha in 2 Kgs 6:19, six times in the northern book Qohelet (2:2, 2:24, 5:15, 5:18, 7:23, 9:13), and in Ezek 40:45. The last passage is once more to be explained by the reunion of northern and
southern exiles in the 6th Century B.C.E. Previous scholars have already commented on the northern origins of the fsg demonstrative
pronoun *zô/zōh*.[13]

Alternatively, *zô* in Ps 132:12 is to be parsed as the relative pronoun, presumably by repointing it to *zû*. This interpretation has been
very common among scholars.[14] If this analysis is accepted, then this
too would be evidence for the northern provenance of the poem (see
above, I.2). Therefore, regardless of which way we understand *zô* in
v. 12, it matters not. Whether as fsg demonstrative pronoun or as relative particle, it is to be included in our list of IH elements.

Summary

The aforementioned points converge to demonstrate that Psalm
132 is a northern composition. In his analysis of this poem, F. M.
Cross concluded that "the traditions of Psalm 132 are wholly inde-

---

[11] D. Hillers, "Ritual Procession of the Ark and Ps 132," *CBQ* 30 (1968) 49–50;
and Cross, *Canaanite Myth and Hebrew Epic*, 95 and n. 20.

[12] Note the following statement (typical of most scholars) by H. Kruse, "Psalm
cxxxii and the Royal Zion Festival," *VT* 33 (1983) 285: "*ʿēdôtî* MT; in correct Hebrew *ʿēdôtay*." In view of the great strides taken in the field of Hebrew dialectology in recent years, scholars should be careful about prescribing "correct"
grammar.

[13] See, e.g., Kutscher, *A History of the Hebrew Language*, 31.

[14] GKC, 109; Joüon, *Grammaire de l'hébreu biblique*, 448; Briggs, *Psalms*, 2. 474;
Kraus, *Psalmen*, 877; etc.

pendent of the traditions in the Deuteronomic history."[15] I would go one step further and claim that this independence results from the chapter's Israelian origin. It is another example of a northern poet who accepted the centrality of Zion in Israelite theology (on this issue see above, pp. 27, 71).

An objection to such a conclusion may be that Psalm 132 is included among the "Songs of Ascent" of chapters 120–134. These poems are almost without doubt to be dated to the post-Exilic period.[16] However, it needs to be pointed out that Psalm 132 is unique among the "Songs of Ascent." While the other fourteen poems are extremely brief, this chapter is relatively long. Furthermore, while the other poems speak about events associated with Second Temple times, Psalm 132 refers back to earlier Israelite history.[17] In light of these differences, there should be no objection to considering this psalm to be an Israelian text.[18] (On the other hand, in the following chapter [see below XIII] we will also argue for the northern provenance of Psalm 133.)

The supposed structural problems of this chapter have led some scholars to conclude that Psalm 132 was originally not a unit.[19] C. Brekelmans has already written a cogent response to this position.[20] In addition to the arguments he presented, we may now advance the evidence of linguistic analysis. Since IH elements span the entire chapter, it renders the theory of redactional disunity of Psalm 132 most improbable.

---

[15] Cross, *Canaanite Myth and Hebrew Epic*, 97. See also McCarter, *II Samuel*, 176–78.

[16] See the standard commentaries. Note as well the linguistic arguments made by Hurvitz (*Beyn Lashon le-Lashon*, 152–163) for Psalms 124, 125, and 133.

[17] These distinctions have been noted recently by C. Stuhlmueller, "Psalms," in *Harper's Bible Commentary* (ed. J. L. Mays; San Francisco: Harper & Row, 1988) 489.

[18] Similarly, the fact that vv. 8–10 are quoted (with slight changes) in 2 Chr 6:41–42 does not militate against our analysis. As an analogy, note the conclusion reached by Welch ("The Source of Nehemiah IX") that Nehemiah 9 originates as a document from the northern kingdom. In other words, though we lack the evidence to reconstruct the history of the transmission of such texts, it was not impossible for the authors of Ezra-Nehemiah and Chronicles to utilize much earlier, northern compositions.

[19] See, e.g., O. Loretz, *Die Psalmen: Beitrag der Ugarit-Texte zum Verständnis von Kolometrie und Textologie der Psalmen*, 2 vols. (AOAT 207; Neukirchen-Vluyn: Neukirchener Verlag, 1979) 2. 292; and K. Seybold, "Die Redaktion der Wallfahrtspsalmen," *ZAW* 91 (1979) 256.

[20] C. Brekelmans, "Psalm 132: Unity and Structure," *Bijdragen, Tijdschirft voor filosofie en theologie* 44 (1983) 262–65.

CHAPTER XIII

Psalm 133

1. The word *nā°îm* "pleasant" in v. 1 is another instance of the use of the root *n°m*. The evidence for the northern distribution of this lexeme was presented in detail earlier (see above II.4).

2. The relative particle *še-* appears twice in this chapter, in vv. 2 and 3. The origin of this form has been widely discussed, but one will agree with Kutscher that "its use was common in the vernacular of Northern Palestine."[1] This conclusion is reached based on the cognate evidence and on the distribution of this morpheme in northern texts. The cognate form *°š* occurs in Phoenician and Ammonite,[2] and perhaps in Deir °Alla.[3]

The form *še-* is found in the following northern compositions[4]: Song of Deborah (Judg 5:7 [bis]), Gideon cycle (Judg 6:17, 7:12, 8:26), Elisha cycle (2 Kgs 6:11 [in the mouth of an Aramean king][5]) Song of Songs (always, except in the superscription in Song 1:1)[6], and Qohelet (67 times). All other instances are in Exilic and post-Exilic compositions (Jon 1:7, 1:12, 4:10, Lam 2:15, 2:16, 4:9, 5:18, Ezra 8:20, 1 Chr 5:20, 27:27, and often in late Psalms). Consequently, we conclude that

---

[1] Kutscher, *A History of the Hebrew Language*, 32.

[2] See Garr, *Dialect Geography*, 85–86. I disagree with the attempt of S. Gevirtz ("On the Etymology of the Phoenician Particle *°š*," *JNES* 16 [1957] 124–27) to disassociate Phoenician *°š* and Hebrew *še-*.

[3] This is the interpretation of Hackett, *The Balaam Text from Deir °Alla*, 31.

[4] I assume that the forms *ša-* and *šā-* are allomorphs of *še-* and thus are to be explained in the same manner.

[5] See Burney, *Kings*, 208.

[6] See Driver, *Introduction*, 449.

še- is northern in origin, and did not penetrate southward until the 6th Century B.C.E.[7]

Accordingly, we can establish a linguistic opposition between IH *še-* and JH *ʾăšer*.[8] The two-fold appearance of the former in Psalm 133, then, is an argument in favor of the northern provenance of this poem.

3. The word *middôtāw* "his garments" in v. 2 is another sign of northern authorship. If we assume that this word is related to other instances of the same root with the same connotation (*middîn, middô-, maddāw*, etc.), then its distribution probably points to this vocable being an IH feature. It appears elsewhere in northern texts in Judg 3:16 (Ehud), 5:10 (Song of Deborah), 1 Sam 8:12 (anonymous Benjaminite), 1 Sam 17:38–39 (Saul), and 1 Sam 18:4 (Jonathan). This leaves only Lev 6:3, 2 Sam 20:8, and Ps 109:18 in Judahite compositions. Cognates to the Hebrew form are found in Aramaic, Ugaritic, and probably Phoenician,[9] thus bolstering this conclusion.

On the other hand, the unique plural form *middôtāw* might suggest distinguishing this word from the aforementioned words. If this route is taken, then we may still appeal to the Ugaritic evidence, for in this language we encounter the plural form *mdt* as well.[10] In either case, we are justified in including the evidence of *middôtāw* in support of our argument for the Israelian origin of Psalm 133.

4. The reference to Mt. Hermon in v. 3 is another indication of this poem's northern orientation.[11] See also above III.1, VI.1, X.1.

---

[7] Even when it did penetrate southward, the evidence suggests that it was limited to colloquial speech. See Rendsburg, *Diglossia in Ancient Hebrew*, 113–18; and earlier Hurvitz, *Beyn Lashon le-Lashon*, 41 n. 94.

[8] Rabin ("Leshonam shel ʿAmos ve-Hosheaʿ," 122) has raised the problem that Hosea only uses *ʾăšer*, never *še-*. If we assume, however, that Hosea's prophecies were centered in Bethel, only a few miles north of Jerusalem, then perhaps *ʾăšer* was the relative pronoun in use there. This contradicts my earlier statement concerning the dialect of Benjamin, but dialect geography teaches us that isoglosses have to be drawn for each particular grammatical and lexical feature. Although the Hebrew of Bethel may have differed from JH in many ways, in the present instance, it may have been linked with JH via their common use of *ʾăšer*. Obviously, lack of a complete picture prevents us from solving this dilemma in a satisfactory way.

[9] For the Aramaic see Jastrow, *Dictionary*, 2.731. For the Ugaritic see Gordon, *Ugaritic Textbook*, 430. For the Phoenician see Tomback, *Phoenician and Punic*, 166.

[10] Gordon, *Ugaritic Textbook*, 430; and Dahood, *Psalms III*, 252.

[11] If I understand him correctly, J. Braslavi ("*kĕṭal ḥermôn šeyyōrēd ʿal harĕrê ṣiyyôn* [Tehillim 133:3]," *Beth Miqra* 49 [1972] 143–45) wishes to denude the refer-

5. The reduplicatory plural form *harĕrê* in v. 3 is an element of IH (see above IV.3).

Summary

These five features in an extremely short poem of only three verses represent a significant bunching of IH traits to justify our labeling this chapter an Israelian poem.[12] The northern provenance of this psalm was noted already by Gunkel and echoed by Dahood.[13] Our analysis fully supports this conclusion.[14] Once more we may note that the mention of Zion (in v. 3) is no reason to deny Israelian authorship to a particular psalm.[15] As I have commented in other instances (I, IX), presumably there were northerners who subscribed to the centrality of Zion in Israelite theology.[16]

---

ence to Hermon here of its northern setting. Instead, he proposes to understand the word as "sacred place" or the like. Although this remains a possibility, the argument is not very convincing. See A. Berlin, "On the Interpretation of Psalm 133," in *Directions in Biblical Hebrew Poetry* [ed. E. R. Follis; JSOTSS 40; Sheffield: JSOT Press, 1987] 141–47, for reasons to affirm the northern connotation of Hermon in v. 3.

[12] Hurvitz (*Beyn Lashon le-Lashon,* 156–60) included Psalm 133 in his list of post-Exilic psalms. The two conclusions (northern and post-Exilic) are not mutually exclusive; see further below, p. 103–4.

[13] Gunkel, *Psalmen,* 571; H. Gunkel, "Psalm 133," in *Karl Budde zum siebzigsten Geburtstag* (ed. K. Marti; BZAW 34; Giessen: Alfred Töpelmann, 1920) 73; and Dahood, *Psalms III,* 250. For discussion see S. Norin, "Ps. 133. Zusammenhang und Datierung," *ASTI* 11 (1977–78) 90–95.

[14] Above (XII) I suggested that Psalm 132 was unique among the Songs of Ascents based on its length and on its content, and therefore perhaps it alone was Israelian in origin. The conclusion that Psalm 133 is also northern forces us to alter that claim. Note, however, that the two poems adjoin each other in the canon. They may have been brought from north to south simultaneously and later gained entry into the final version of Psalms in adjacent positions. Such machinations lead us into the world of speculation, however.

[15] The emendation proposed by E. Power ("Şion or Si'on in Psalm 133 [Vulg 132])," *Biblica* 3 [1922] 342–49) to read the mountain name *śî'ōn* "Sion" (= Hermon in Deut 4:48) in place of *şiyyôn* "Zion" is very ingenious, but it has no support. Furthermore, see the next note for making sense of the mention of Zion in this psalm.

[16] Furthermore, Berlin ("On the Interpretation of Psalm 133") has adduced literary factors as to how and why Hermon and Zion interact in v. 3. I much prefer Berlin's interpretation to that of Z. Zevit ("Psalms on the Poetic Precipice," *HAR* 10 [1986] 351–66) which views Psalm 133 as an example of sloppy poetry.

CHAPTER XIV

Psalm 140

1. Above (VIII.9) I noted that *pa'am* "foot" is a northern vocable. Accordingly, its appearance in v. 5 is an indication of the Israelian provenance of this psalm.

2. Another northern vocable is the noun *ḥēmāh* "venom, poison," treated above (VIII.4). Thus its occurrence in v. 4 (in the singular construct *ḥămat*) is also a sign of this poem's northern origin.

3. In v. 9 the word *ma'ăwayyê* "desires of" is a nominal form derived from a IIIy verb *'wy* with the *yod* retained. Above (IV.4) we concluded that this is an IH feature.[1]

4. The root *pwq* in the Hiph'il occurs in v. 9 with the meaning "obtain, meet." This verb appears in Ugaritic[2] and Phoenician[3] and in four instances in the northern book of Proverbs (3:13, 8:35, 12:2, 18:22).[4] The other two biblical attestations are in post-Exilic compositions (Isa 58:10, Ps 144:13), where IH influence may be suspected.[5]

---

[1] Dahood (*Psalms III*, 303) labeled this an archaism, which is only partially correct. Briggs (*Psalms*, 2.503) considered this word an Aramaism, though it is not clear to me on what grounds.

[2] Gordon, *Ugaritic Textbook*, 467. See further Gray, *The Krt Text in the Literature of Ras Shamra*, 31.

[3] It appears in *KAI* 50:3. The word is not listed in Tomback, *Phoenician and Punic*, though he did include the noun *pqt* (p. 271) which seems to mean "profit" and is probably related.

[4] For general discussion see M. Greenberg, "Mizmor 140," *Eretz-Israel* 14 (H. L. Ginsberg Volume) (1978) 91.

[5] I exclude from this treatment the two attestations of *pwq* "totter, stagger" in Isa 28:7, Jer 10:4.

The evidence prompts me to conclude that *pwq* "obtain, meet" is an IH vocable.

5. The *hapax legomenon mahămōrôt* "deep pits" in v. 11 is explained only via its Ugaritic cognate *mhmrt*.[6] Although scholars disagree on minor details concerning the identification of these two terms, all agree that they are related.[7] Consequently, we may recognize in *mahămōrôt* another IH element.

6. The context of v. 11 makes it very clear that the preposition *b* in this passage must be translated "from."[8] The phrase *bĕmahămōrôt bal yāqûmû* can only mean "from the deep pits they will not arise." This usage was treated above (I.3) and recognized as a characteristic of IH.

7. The negative particle *bal* (see above I.5) occurs twice in this poem, in vv. 11 and 12.

8. The spelling *ydᶜt* in the Kethiv of v. 13, which appears in the Qere as *yādaᶜtî* "I know," reflects Phoenician orthography.[9] A similar example appears in another northern poem, Ps 16:2 (see above II.2).[10]

Summary

This psalm includes eight indications of IH. These are deemed to represent a sufficient quantity of northern features to conclude that Psalm 140 originates in northern Israel. Furthermore, it is probably not coincidental that the next chapter, Psalm 141, is another northern poem (see below XV). Though it cannot be proved beyond doubt, it is

---

[6] Gordon, *Ugaritic Textbook*, 391.

[7] The bibliography of these two words and the related Ugaritic word *hmry* is vast. Consult the following: R. Dussaud, "Le Mythe de Ba'al et d'Aliyan d'après des documents nouveaux," *Revue de l'histoire des religions* 111 (1935) 33 n. 4; G. Widengren, "Review of M. Seligson, *The Meaning of npš mt in the Old Testament*," *VT* 4 (1954) 98–99; U. Cassuto, "Baal and Mot in the Ugaritic Texts," *IEJ* 12 (1962) 81; Dahood, *Psalms III*, 305; M. Held, "Pits and Pitfalls in Akkadian and Biblical Hebrew," *JANES* 5 (1973) 188; M. H. Pope, "A Little Soul-Searching," *Maarav* 1 (1978) 25–31; and Greenberg, "Mizmor 140," 93.

[8] As noted by Dahood, *Psalms III*, 305.

[9] This is a better explanation than the one offered by GKC, 121, and by Greenberg ("Mizmor 140," 94 n. 34), that the Kethiv represents an older orthography before the introduction of vowel letters.

[10] Dahood, *Psalms III*, 306.

most likely that these two compositions are juxtaposed in the biblical canon due to their common origin in the northern region of Israel.

CHAPTER XV

Psalm 141

1. The *hapax legomenon dal* in v. 3 means "door," i.e., it is a variant form of the standard Hebrew term *delet*. It was thus interpreted by the LXX and by virtually all commentators and translators since then.[1] Since the form *dl* occurs in Phoenician as the word for "door,"[2] we follow Dahood in concluding that *dal* in Ps 141:3 is a northern feature.[3]

2. The atypical plural form *ʾîšîm* "men" occurs in v. 4. This too corresponds to the Phoenician form, which is written *ʾšm.*[4] Elsewhere in the Bible, *ʾîšîm* appears in Isa 53:3, Prov 8:4.[5] The latter passage returns us once more to the early chapters of Proverbs replete with many northernisms. The former reference may be explained by Gordon's hypothesis on the influence of IH on exilic and post-Exilic compositions.

3. The negative particle *bal* is used in v. 4. This feature of IH has appeared in many of the poems discussed above (I.5, II.1, VI.8, VIII.8, X.15, XIV.7).

4. The verb *lḥm* "eat" appears in v. 4. This usage is rare in Hebrew, attested to elsewhere in Prov 4:17, 9:5, 23:1, 23:6, and probably Deut 32:24.[6] The four attestations in Proverbs place us once more in a

---

[1] See, e.g., Briggs, *Psalms*, 2.507, 510; Buttenweiser, *Psalms,* 735; and Kraus, *Psalmen*, 2.927, 929.

[2] Tomback (*Phoenician and Punic,* 71) cites only the plural form *dlht.* For the singular *dl*, see Friedrich and Röllig, *Phönizisch-punische Grammatik*, 116.

[3] Dahood, *Psalm III*, 310. See also Kraus, *Psalmen*, 2.929.

[4] Tomback, *Phoenician and Punic*, 33.

[5] Rendsburg, "Morphological Evidence."

[6] See Rendsburg, "Northern Origin," 117 and n. 32.

northern book. The passage in Deuteronomy 32 is *lĕḥūmê rešep*, which may mean "attacked by Reshef" or "consumed by Reshef." If it is the former, this example is not germane. If it is the latter, or if it is a case of polysemy as seems likely, then we have another instance of *lḥm* "eat" in a northern poem (on Deuteronomy 32, see above, p. 12). Moreover, note that *lḥm* is the commonest verb in Ugaritic for "eat."[7]

5.   The word *manʿammêhem* "their delicacies" in v. 4 is another *hapax legomenon* paralleled in Phoenician. It occurs four times in the Karatepe inscription.[8] Clearly, it must have been a word known in northern Israel, but which did not enter into the Judahite lexicon.

6.   In v. 5 we encounter once more the root *hlm* "strike" in *yehelmēnî* "let him strike me." Above (IX.5) we isolated this verb as a trait of IH.

7.   The unusual form *yānî* in v. 5 has been the source of much discussion among scholars.[9] Here I would like to propose a novel analysis which will be consistent with this poem's northern provenance. The word *yānî* is to be understood as "my wine," reflecting the contraction of the diphthong well-known to be characteristic of northern Hebrew. However, I do not believe that we need to alter the vocalization to *yênî*.

Instead, let it be noted that monophthongization of *aw/ay > ā* occurs in a number of places in Hebrew and elsewhere, all of which indicates a northern locale for this shift. In a recent lengthy article I have reviewed the evidence from Eblaite, Amorite, Ugaritic, Amarna, and colloquial Syro-Lebanese Arabic,[10] and W. R. Garr has similarly gathered the material from Aramaic.[11] Here I shall only briefly mention a few of the examples from Hebrew.

In 1 Sam 10:14, 2 Kgs 5:25, Job 8:2 the interrogative *ʾān* occurs instead of expected *ʾayin*. The first of these is in the mouth of Saul's un-

---

[7]   Gordon, *Ugaritic Textbook*, 427.

[8]   Tomback, *Phoenician and Punic*, 187.

[9]   Note the comment of Buttenweiser (*Psalms*, 738): "The third stich of verse 5 of Psalm 141 is so hopelessly corrupt that it does not admit of either translation or emendation." For an attempt to explain the form see Driver, "Textual and Linguistic Problems in the Book of Psalms," 193.

[10]   G. A. Rendsburg, "Monophthongization of *aw/ay > ā* in Eblaite and in Northwest Semitic," in *Eblaitica: Essays on the Ebla Archives and Eblaite Language*, Vol. 2 (eds. C. H. Gordon and G. A. Rendsburg; Winona Lake, IN: Eisenbrauns, 1990) 91–126.

[11]   W. R. Garr, "**ay > a* in Targum Onqelos," *JAOS* (forthcoming). I am grateful to Professor Garr for permitting me to see his article in manuscript form.

cle, presumably a Benjaminite, the second is spoken by Elisha, and the third is in a book with a Transjordanian setting. Similarly, in Job 9:9 occurs the form *ʿāš*, probably Ursa Major,[12] corresponding to *ʿayiš* in Job 38:32 and probably connected with Arabic *ġayṯ* "rain."[13] Compare as well the northern place name *dōtān* vs. *dōtāynāh* in Gen 37:17, 2 Kgs 6:13.

The meaning "my wine" for *yānî* in Ps 141:5 fits the context perfectly. In this passage it is parallel to *šemen* "oil," as is also the case in Amos 6:6, Mic 6:15, Ps 104:15, Song 1:2–3, 4:10 (see also Deut 28:39–40, Prov 21:17, 2 Chr 11:11).[14] In short, I consider *yānî* in our passage to be a dialectal northern equivalent to standard BH *yênî*.

8. The root *nʿm* occurs not only in *manʿammêhem* in v. 4 but also in *nāʿēmû* "are sweet" in v. 6.[15] Above (II.4) we noted that this root was used much more commonly in the north than in Judah.

Summary

More than half a century ago, W. F. Albright wrote as follows: "Dr. H. L. Ginsberg has been particularly active in identifying Phoenician or Canaanite elements in the Psalter. He kindly gives me permission to mention his latest observation, that the language of

---

[12] M. H. Pope, *Job* (AB 15; Garden City, NY: Doubleday, 1973) 68, 71; and R. Gordis, *The Book of Job* (New York: Jewish Theological Seminary, 1978) 96, 104.

[13] G. R. Driver, "Two Astronomical Passages in the Old Testament," *JTS* 7 (1956) 2. On the connection between stars and rain among the peoples of antiquity, as evidenced in passages such as Judg 5:20 and *UT* ʿnt:II:41 as well as various Greek and Roman texts, see T. H. Gaster, *Thespis* (New York: Gordian, 1975) 237; J. Blenkinsopp, "Ballad Style and Psalm Style in the Song of Deborah: A Discussion," *Biblica* 42 (1961) 73; and R. G. Boling, *Judges* (AB 6A; Garden City, NY: Doubleday, 1975) 113.

[14] For discussion and for the two cognates in Ugaritic in parallelism see Dahood, "Ugaritic-Hebrew Parallel Pairs," 210; and Avishur, *Stylistic Studies of Word-Pairs*, 367–68. D. Gualandi ("Salmo 141 [140]," *RBI* 6 [1958] 220 n. 9) called attention to the similarity between Ps 141:5 and Prov 27:9 *šemen ûqĕṭōret yĕśammaḥ lēb* "oil and spice gladden the heart." The latter verse, in turns, recalls Ps 104:15 *wĕyayin yĕśammaḥ lĕbab ʾĕnôš* "and wine gladden the heart of man." This evidence is another way of indicating the pairing of *šemen* "oil" and *yayin* "wine."

[15] R. J. Tournay, "Psaume CXLI: Nouvelle interpretation," *RB* 90 (1983) 327, has made the acute observation that the roots *nʿm* and *lḥm* appear together not only in Ps 141:4 but also in Prov 9:17. The latter verse places us once more in a composition with many Phoenician affinities.

Psalm 141 contains a number of characteristically Phoenician words and forms."[16] Tournay also perceived that Psalm 141 includes many parallels to Phoenician.[17] Dahood went further, specifying "the Phoenician territory as the probable place of this poem's composition."[18] Our investigation has borne these judgments out, though I would adjust Dahood's statement to suggest the northern territory of Israel as the provenance of this chapter.[19] Moreover, as noted at the end of the last chapter (see above XIV), it is likely that Psalms 140 and 141 appear side-by-side in the canon due to their common place of origin in northern Israel.

---

[16] W. F. Albright, "Recent Progress in North-Canaanite Research," *BASOR* 70 (1938) 23–24 n. 22.

[17] R. Tournay, "Le psaume cxli," *VT* 9 (1959) 63.

[18] Dahood, *Psalms III,* 309.

[19] It is probably only a coincidence that the expression in Ps 141:7 *nipzĕrû ʿăṣāmênû* "our bones are scattered" is paralleled in the northern Ps 53:6 *pizzar ʿaṣmôt* "scattered the bones," a phrase which is lacking in the parallel southern Psalm 14 (on these two chapters see above VII). On the other hand, a direct relationship is proposed by R. Weiss, "Textual Notes," *Textus* 6 (1968) 131. For a nexus between this verse and Ugaritic literature see J. B. Burns, "An Interpretation of Psalm cxli 7b," *VT* 22 (1972) 245–46.

CONCLUSION

In the foregoing fifteen chapters, linguistic evidence has been presented to demonstrate the northern origin of selected psalms. The following poems evince a sufficient concentration of northern grammatical and lexical features to merit the conclusion that they originated in northern Israel: Psalms 9–10, 16, 29, 36, 45, 53, 58, 74, 116, 132, 133, 140, 141. In addition, the collections of poems ascribed to Korah (Psalms 42–49, 84–85, 87–88) and to Asaph (Psalms 50, 73–83) show a similar concentration of northern traits, enough to justify their inclusion in this study. The total number of Psalms is thus 36 out of 150, or 24%, where northern provenance is demonstrable.

Thus far I have not discussed the dating of these poems. It is probable, for obvious reasons, that most of these psalms were composed before 721 B.C.E. But this cannot be proved. Indeed, one could argue that they date from after the downfall of the northern kingdom of Israel. Earlier (above, p. 12) I noted the evidence for the continued existence of Israelians in northern Israel after 721 B.C.E. Moreover, segments of this population are portrayed as being loyal to Jerusalem. Stories such as those in 2 Chronicles 30 and Jer 41:4–5 could easily serve as the context for the authorship of many of the northern psalms with their Zion-based theology. Even Psalm 78, whose purpose is to argue that Zion and the Davidic dynasty are now replacing Shiloh, could fit into this scheme. Note that Shiloh is specifically mentioned in Jer 41:5.

I have no doubt that IH continued to be used in Samaria, Galilee, and Gilead after 721 B.C.E. The presence of Phoenician, Aramaic, Moabite, etc., would have continued to create the same or similar isoglosses, regardless of Samaria's defeat. In fact, this is true not only for the century or two immediately following the downfall of the kingdom of Israel, but for all of antiquity into Persian, Hellenistic, and Roman times as well.[1] Accordingly, it is very possible for an individual psalm's language to contain both northern elements and characteristics of LBH. Such a poem is Psalm 133 (see above, XIII [especially p. 93, n. 12]).

In conclusion, it is probable that most of the northern psalms treated in this monograph date from before 721 B.C.E., but this is by no means certain. It is possible for any or many of them to date from after 721 B.C.E.

It is conceivable that still other chapters in the book of Psalms await a determination of northern origin, though I must add that it is most unlikely. My study of the remaining 114 chapters has failed to yield another example of a poem with a significant concentration of IH characteristics. For example, in Ps 4:3 we encounter another instance of *meh* before a non-laryngeal consonant (see above I.6), but this poem is devoid of any additional northern elements. Similarly, Psalm 104 contains three uses of the negative particle *bal* (I.5), but there is no concentration of northern features in this psalm either.

Even northern toponymy is not a sure indication of northern origin. Psalm 89 is a case in point, for Mt. Tabor and Mt. Hermon are mentioned in v. 13. But the chapter has not even a single example of an unquestionable IH feature, and even Briggs was able to posit only one Aramaism in this relatively long psalm.[2] Moreover, in his famous essay on this poem, Sarna proved that its background is thoroughly Judahite.[3] The poem which comes closest to meriting inclusion in this study is Psalm 103, which displays some peculiar grammatical usages. But here I concur with Hurvitz's interpretation of the data that the psalm is post-exilic and probably Judahite in origin.[4]

In conclusion, there are 36 poems in the book of Psalms wherein linguistic evidence points very clearly to northern provenance. The ramifications of this finding for historical, theological, and redactional research, to mention only several areas of related interest, I leave for others to explore.

---

[1] The Galilean origin of Mishnaic Hebrew would fit into this picture as well. On the many links between the language of the Mishna, on the one hand, and Phoenician and Aramaic, on the other hand, see Rendsburg, "The Galilean Background of Mishnaic Hebrew."

[2] Briggs, *Psalms*, 2.266. The example is *ḥāsîn* in v. 9, though even here the evidence is not compelling.

[3] N. M. Sarna, "Psalm 89: A Study in Inner Biblical Exegesis," in *Biblical and Other Studies* (ed. A. Altmann; Cambridge: Harvard University Press, 1963) 29–46.

[4] Hurvitz, *Beyn Lashon le-Lashon*, 107–30.

APPENDIX

Features of Israelian Hebrew Isolated in This Study
(Citations are by chapter and section)

I. Phonology
   A. Consonants
      1. PS *ḍ* represented by ʿ (not *ṣ̌*) (I.1)
   B. Vowels
      1. Shift of *a* to *ō* (VI.13; see also "Feminine singular nominal ending -*ôt*," below under Morphology)
   C. Diphthongs
      1. Monophthongization of *ay* > *ā* (XV.7)

II. Orthography
      1. Defective writing of 1csg perfect ending -*tî* (II.2, XIV.8)

III. Morphology
   A. Pronouns
      1. 2fsg pronominal suffix -*kî* (XI.2)
      2. 3msg pronominal suffix -*ôhî* (XI.5)
      3. Relative pronoun *zeh/zû* (I.2, IX.1, X.17)
      4. Relative pronoun *še-* (XIII.2)
      5. Feminine singular demonstrative pronoun *zô* (XII.7)
      6. Interrogative pronoun *meh* before non-laryngeal consonants (I.6)
   B. Nouns
      1. Feminine singular nominal ending -*at* (I.4, II.3, VI.14, VII.2, IX.8, XII.2)
      2. Feminine singular nominal ending -*ôt* (II.6, V.1, VI.7, VII.1, VIII.1, X.8, XII.6; see also "Shift of *a* to *ō*," above under Phonology)
      3. Reduplicatory plural of geminate noun (IV.3, VI.12, X.3, XIII.5)

      4. ʾēšet "woman" in absolute state (VIII.7)

C. Verbs

      1. Retention of *yod* in IIIy verbs and derived nouns (IV.4, X.4, XIV.3)

      2. Retention of *he* in imperfect, infinitive, and imperative forms of *hlk* (VIII.6)

      3. Non-elision of *he* in Hiphʿil and Hophʿal forms (V.8, X.22, XI.1)

      4. ʾEtpolel conjugation (X.11)

      5. 3msg imperfect in *t-* (VI.2)

D. Particles

      1. Prepositions *b/l* "from" (I.3, III.4, XII.5, XIV.6)

      2. Non-elision of definite article *he* after uniconsonantal prepositions *b, l, k* (IV.2)

      3. Root *yrʾ* governed by preposition *b-* (not *m-*) (VI.5)

      4. Negative particle *bal* (I.5, II.1, VI.8, VIII.8, X.15, XIV.7, XV.3)

      5. Conjunction *p-* "and" (VI.10, X.2)

IV. Syntax

      1. Progressive tense (I.7)

      2. "Double plural" (III.2, V.6, VI.9, IX.6, X.12, XI.3)

V. Lexicon

A. Nouns and Adjectives

      1. Divine epithet *ʾăbîr yaʿăqōb* (XII.1)

      2. *ʾûl* "strength, body" (X.5)

      3. *ʾîšîm* "men" (XV.2)

      4. *dal* "door" (XV.1)

      5. *hêkāl* "palace" (V.5)

      6. *ḥēleb* "hill" (X.23)

      7. *ḥēmāh* "venom, poison" (VIII.4, XIV.2)

      8. *ḥmr* "wine" (X.9)

      9. Plural form *yĕʿārôt* "forests" (III.3)

     10. *yāqār* "grievous" (XI.6)

     11. *yĕqār* " honor " (VI.11)

     12. *kannāh* "stem, stalk, root" (X.18)

     13. *keseh* "full moon" (X.20)

     14. *kaššîl* "hatchet" (IX.4)

     15. *middôt* "garments" (XIII.3)

     16. *māhîr* "skillful " (V.3)

     17. *mahămōrôt* "deep pits" (XIV.5)

18. *malkût* "kingdom" (V.4)
19. *man⁽ammêhem* "their delicacies" (XV.5; see also *n⁽m* below)
20. *mesek* "mixed wine" (X.10)
21. Plural construct *miškĕnê* "tabernacles" (VI.6)
22. *miškĕnôt* "tabernacle" with singular connotation (VI.3, X.13, XII.3)
23. *n⁽m* "good" (II.4, X.21, XIII.1, XV.8; see also *man⁽ammêhem* above)
24. *pa⁽am* "foot" (VIII.9, XIV.1)
25. *peten* "viper, serpent" (VIII.5)
26. *qardum-* "axe" (IX.3)
27. *špr* "good, beautiful" (II.5)

B. Verbs
1. *dbr* "carry off, pursue" (XI.4)
2. *dwr* "dwell" (VI.15)
3. *hlm* "strike" (IX.5, XV.6)
4. *yd⁽* "smite" (IX.2)
5. *ksḥ* "cut down" (X.19)
6. *lḥm* "eat" (XV.4)
7. *mwq* "mock" (X.6)
8. *nĕ'ûm* "spoken" predicated of humans (IV.1)
9. H-stem *pwq* "obtain, meet" (XIV.4)
10. *pls* "weigh, make level, straighten" (VIII.3, X.16)
11. *p⁽l* "do, make, work" (VI.4, VIII.2)
12. *rḥš* "astir" (V.2)
13. *šnn* "cry, weep, lament" (X.7)
14. H-stem *twh* "grieve" (X.14)

VI. Word pairs
1. Word pairs shared with Phoenician
    a. *brk/ntn* (III.5)
    b. *n⁽m/šb⁽* (II.7)
2. Word pairs shared with Ugaritic (III.6)

VII. Miscellaneous
1. Toponymy (III.1, VI.1, IX.7, X.1, XII.4, XIII.4)
2. *bat ṣûr* "daughter of Tyre" (VI.7)

BIBLIOGRAPHY

Aartun, K. "Textüberlieferung und vermeintliche Belege der Konjunktion *pV* im Alten Testament," *UF* 10 (1978) 1–13.

Aistleitner, J. *Wörterbuch der ugaritischen Sprache.* Berlin: Akadamie Verlag, 1963.

Albright, W. F. "A Catalogue of Early Hebrew Lyric Poems (Psalm LXVIII)," *HUCA* 23/1 (1950–51) 1–39.

_____. "New Light on Early Canaanite Language and Literature," *BASOR* 46 (1932) 15–20.

_____. "Recent Progress in North-Canaanite Research," *BASOR* 70 (1938) 18–24.

_____. "Some Canaanite-Phoenician Sources of Hebrew Wisdom," in *Wisdom in Israel and in the Ancient Near East.* Eds. M. Noth, and D. W. Thomas. SVT 3. Leiden: E. J. Brill, 1960. Pp. 1–15.

_____. *Yahweh and the Gods of Canaan.* London: School of Oriental and African Studies, 1968.

Astour, M. C. "Two Ugaritic Serpent Charms," *JNES* 27 (1968) 13–36.

Avigad, N. "An Inscribed Bowl from Dan," *PEQ* 100 (1968) 42–44.

Avishur, Y. "Le-Ziqa ha-Signonit Beyn Shir ha-Shirim ve-Sifrut ʾUgarit," *Beth Miqra* 59 (1974) 508–25.

_____. *Stylistic Studies of Word-Pairs in Biblical and Ancient Semitic Literatures.* AOAT 210. Neukirchen-Vluyn: Neukirchener Verlag, 1984.

_____. "*Wekilyôtay ʾeštônān* (Tehillim 73:21)," *Leshonenu* 44 (1979–80) 263–67.

Barr, J. *Comparative Philology and the Text of the Old Testament.* Oxford: Clarendon, 1968.

Bauer, H., and P. Leander. *Historische Grammatik der hebräischen Sprache des Alten Testamentes.* Halle: Max Niemeyer, 1922.

Bendavid, A. *Leshon ha-Miqra³ u-Lshon Ḥakhamim.* 2 vols. Tel Aviv: Dvir, 1967–71.

_____. *Maqbilot ba-Miqra³.* Jerusalem: Carta, 1972.

Benz, F. L. *Personal Names in the Phoenician and Punic Inscriptions.* Rome: Pontifical Biblical Institute, 1972.

Bergsträsser, G. *Hebräische Grammatik.* Leipzig: F. C. W. Vogel, 1918.

Berlin, A. "On the Interpretation of Psalm 133," in *Directions in Biblical Hebrew Poetry.* Ed. E. R. Follis. JSOTSS 40. Sheffield: JSOT Press, 1987. Pp. 141–47.

Blau, J. *A Grammar of Biblical Hebrew.* Wiesbaden: Otto Harrassowitz, 1976.

Blenkinsopp, J. "Ballad Style and Psalm Style in the Song of Deborah: A Discussion," *Biblica* 42 (1961) 61–76.

Blommerde, A. C. M. *Northwest Semitic Grammar and Job.* Rome: Pontifical Biblical Institute, 1969.

Boling, R. G. *Judges.* AB 6A. Garden City, NY: Doubleday, 1975.

Braslavi, J. "Kĕṭal ḥermôn šeyyôrēd ʿal harĕrê ṣiyyôn (Tehillim 133:3)," *Beth Miqra* 49 (1972) 143–45.

Brekelmans, C. "Psalm 132: Unity and Structure," *Bijdragen, Tijdschrift voor filosofie en theologie* 44 (1983) 262–65.

Briggs, C. A. *A Critical and Exegetical Commentary on the Book of Psalms.* 2 vols. ICC. New York: Charles Scribner's Sons, 1906–07.

Brown, F., S. R. Driver, and C. A. Briggs. *A Hebrew and English Lexicon of the Old Testament.* Oxford: Clarendon Press, 1906.

Brown, J. P. "The Mediterranean Vocabulary of the Vine," *VT* 19 (1969) 146–70.

Budde, K. "Psalm 14 and 53," *JBL* 47 (1928) 160–83.

Burney, C. F. *The Book of Judges.* London: Rivingtons, 1918.

_____. *Notes on the Hebrew Text of the Books of Kings.* Oxford: Clarendon Press, 1903.

Burns, J. B. "An Interpretation of Psalm cxli 7b," *VT* 22 (1972) 245–46.

Buss, M. J. "The Psalms of Asaph and Korah," *JBL* 82 (1963) 382–92.

Buttenweiser, M. *The Psalms.* Chicago: University of Chicago Press, 1938.

Campbell, A. F. "Psalm 78: A Contribution to the Theology of Tenth Century Israel," *CBQ* 41 (1979) 51–79.

Caquot, A. "Le psaume lxxiii," *Semitica* 21 (1971) 29–55.

_____. "Une inscription araméene d'époque assyrienne," in *Homages à Andre Dupont-Sommer*. Paris: Maisonneuve, 1971. Pp. 9–16.

Carroll, R. P. "Psalm lxxviii: Vestiges of a Tribal Polemic," *VT* 21 (1971) 133–50.

Casetti, P. *Gibt es ein Leben vor dem Tod?* OBO 44. Göttingen: Vandenhoeck & Ruprecht, 1982.

Caspari, W. "Psalm 84 in drei Strophen," *ZDMG* 75 (1921) 51–56.

Cassuto, U. (M.D.). "Baal and Mot in the Ugaritic Texts," *IEJ* 12 (1962) 77–86.

_____. "ᵓEprat, ᵓEpratah," *EM* 1 (1950) 515–16.

Cavalletti, S. "Il dio ebbro di vino," *Ricerche Bibliche e Religiose* 15 (1981) 135–36.

_____. "Proposta di lettura del Sal. 78,65," *RBI* 26 (1978) 337–40.

Chambers, J. K., and P. Trudgill. *Dialectology*. Cambridge: Cambridge University Press, 1980.

Chomsky, W. *Hebrew: The Eternal Language*. Philadelphia: Jewish Publication Society, 1964.

Cogan, M., and H. Tadmor. *II Kings*. AB 11. Garden City, NY: Doubleday, 1988.

Cohen, A. *The Psalms*. London: Soncino, 1945.

Cohen, H. R. (C.). *Biblical Hapax Legomena in the Light of Akkadian and Ugaritic*. SBLDS 37. Missoia, MT: Scholars Press, 1978.

Corre, A. D. "ᵓēlle, hēmma = sic," *Biblica* 54 (1973) 263–64.

Cowley, A. E. *Aramaic Papyri of the Fifth Century B.C.* Oxford: Clarendon Press, 1923.

Cross, F. M. *Canaanite Myth and Hebrew Epic*. Cambridge, MA: Harvard University Press, 1973.

_____. "Notes on a Canaanite Psalm in the Old Testament," *BASOR* 117 (1950) 19–21.

Dahood, M. "Canaanite-Phoenician Influence in Qoheleth," *Biblica* 33 (1952) 30–52, 191–221.

_____. "Hebrew-Ugaritic Lexicography III," *Biblica* 46 (1965) 311–32.

_____. "The Language and Date of Psalm 48 (47)," *CBQ* 16 (1954) 15–19.

_____. "The Language of Qoheleth," *CBQ* 14 (1952) 227–32.

_____. "The Phoenician Background of Qoheleth," *Biblica* 47 (1966) 264–82.

_____. *Psalms I.* AB 16. Garden City, NY: Doubleday, 1966.

_____. *Psalms II.* AB 17. Garden City, NY: Doubleday, 1968.

_____. *Psalms III.* AB 17A. Garden City, NY: Doubleday, 1970.

_____. "Some Northwest-Semitic Words in Job," *Biblica* 38 (1957) 306–20.

_____. "Ugaritic-Hebrew Parallel Pairs," in *Ras Shamra Parallels.* 3 vols. Eds. L. R. Fisher (and S. Rummel). AnOr 49–51. Rome: Pontifical Biblical Institute, 1972–81. 1.71–382.

_____. *Ugaritic-Hebrew Philology.* Rome: Pontifical Biblical Institute, 1965.

Dalman, G. "Zu Psalm 42, 7. 8," *PJB* (1909) 101–103.

Davila, J. R. "Qoheleth and Northern Hebrew," in *Sopher Mahir: Northwest Semitic Studies Presented to Stanislav Segert = Maarav 5–6* (1990) 69–87.

Day, J. "Shear-Jashub (Isaiah vii 3) and 'The Remnant of Wrath' (Psalm lxxvi 11)," *VT* 31 (1981) 76–78.

Decamps de Mertzenfeld, C. *Inventaire commenté des ivoires phéniciens et apparentés, découverts dans le Proche Orient, Texte.* Paris: E. de Boccard, 1954.

Degen, R. *Altaramäische Grammatik.* Wiesbaden: Franz Steiner, 1969.

van Dijk, H. J. "Does Third Masciine *taqtul* Exist in Hebrew?" *VT* 19 (1969) 440–47.

Dinaburg, B. Z. "Pereq bi-Thillim mi-Zemano shel Hosheaᶜ ben Elah," *Qoveṣ ha-Ḥevra ha-ᶜIvrit le-Ḥaqirat ᵓEreṣ Yiśraᵓel ve-ᵓAtiqoteha (= JJPES)* (1928) 250–61.

Donner, H. "Ugaritismen in der Psalmenforschung," *ZAW* 79 (1967) 322–50.

Dotan, A. "Stress Position and Vowel Shift in Phoenician and Punic," *IOS* 6 (1976) 71–121.

Driver, G. R. "Hebrew Studies," *JRAS* (1948) 164–76.

_____. "Studies on the Vocabulary of the Old Testament. VII," *JTS* 35 (1934) 380–93.

_____. "Textual and Linguistic Problems of the Book of Psalms," *HTR* 29 (1936) 171–95.

_____. "Two Astronomical Passages in the Old Testament," *JTS* 7 (1956) 1–11.

Driver, S. R. *An Introduction to the Literature of the Old Testament.* New York: Charles Scribner's Sons, 1906.

_____. *Notes on the Hebrew Text of the Books of Samuel.* Oxford: Clarendon, 1890.

_____. *A Treatise on the Use of the Tenses in Hebrew.* Oxford: Clarendon, 1892.

Dussaud, R. "Le Mythe de Ba'al et d'Aliyan d'après des documents nouveaux," *Revue de l'histoire des religions* 111 (1935) 5–65.

Ebeling, E. "Das Verbum der El-Amarna-Briefe," *BASS* 8 (1910) 39–79.

Eissfeldt, O. *Kleine Schriften.* 6 vols. Tübingen: J. C. B. Mohr, 1962–79.

_____. *Das Lied Moses Deuteronomium 32,1–43 und das Lehrgedicht Asaphs Psalm 78 samt einer Analyse der Umgebung des Mose-Liedes.* Berichte über die Verhandlugen der Sächsischen Akademie der Wissenschaften zu Leipzig, Philologisch-historische Klasse, Band 104, Heft 5. Berlin: Akademie-Verlag, 1958.

_____. *The Old Testament: An Introduction.* New York: Harper and Row, 1965.

_____. "Psalm 76," *TLZ* 82 (1957) 801–8.

_____. "Psalm 80," in *Geschichte und Altes Testament: Albrecht Alt zum 70. Geburtstag dargebracht.* Tübingen: J. C. B. Mohr, 1953.

_____. "Psalm 80 und Psalm 89," *WO* 3 (1964–66) 27–31.

_____. "Psalm 132," *WO* 2 (1954–59) 480–83.

Elliger, K., and W. Rudolph, eds. *Biblia Hebraica Stuttgartensia.* Stuttgart: Deutsche Bibelstiftung, 1977.

Emerton, J. A. "How Does the Lord Regard the Death of His Saints in Psalm cxvi 15," *JTS* 84 (1983) 146–56.

_____. "A Neglected Solution of a Problem in Psalm lxxvi 11," *VT* 24 (1974) 136–46.

_____. "Notes on Three Passages in Psalms Book III," *JTS* 14 (1963) 374–81.

_____. "'Spring and Torrent' in Psalm lxxiv 15," *Volume du Congrès: Genève 1965.* SVT 15. Leiden: E. J. Brill, 1966. Pp. 122–33.

Eph'al, I. *The Ancient Arabs.* Jerusalem: Magnes, 1982.

Fenton, T. L. "Gishot Shonot shel Sifre ha-Miqra' le-Mitos ha-Te'omakiya," in *Studies in Bible and the Ancient Near East Presented to Samuel E. Loewenstamm.* Eds. Y. Avishur and J. Blau. Jerusalem: E. Rubinstein, 1978. Pp. 337–81.

Ferguson, C. A. "Diglossia," *Word* 15 (1959) 325–40.

Finkelstein, I. *The Archaeology of the Israelite Settlement.* Jerusalem: Israel Exploration Society, 1988.

Fishman, J. A. "Bilingualism With and Without Diglossia; Diglossia With and Without Bilingualism," *Journal of Social Issues* 23 (1967) 29–38.

_____. "The Sociology of Language," in *Current Trends in Linguistics.* 14 volumes. Ed. T. A. Sebeok. The Hague: Mouton, 1963–1976. Pp. 12.1629–1784.

Fitzmyer, J. A. *The Aramaic Inscriptions of Sefire.* Rome: Pontifical Biblical Institute, 1967.

Fox, M. V. *The Song of Songs and the Ancient Egyptian Love Songs.* Madison: University of Wisconsin Press, 1985.

Freedman, D. N. "Divine Names and Titles in Early Hebrew Poetry," in *Magnalia Dei: The Mighty Acts of God: Essays on the Bible and Archaeology in Memory of G. Ernest Wright.* Eds. F. M. Cross, W. E. Lemke, and P. D. Miller. Garden City, NY: Doubleday, 1976. Pp. 55–107.

_____. "Orthographic Peculiarities in the Book of Job," *Eretz-Israel* 9 (W. F. Albright Volume) (1969) 35–44.

_____. *Pottery, Poetry, and Prophecy.* Winona Lake, IN: Eisenbrauns, 1986.

Freehof, S. B. "Sound the Shofar—'Ba-Kesse' Psalm 81:4," *JQR* 64 (1973–74) 225–28.

Fretheim, T. E. "Psalm 132: A Form-Critical Study," *JBL* 86 (1967) 289–300.

Friedrich, J., and W. Röllig. *Phönizisch-punische Grammatik.* 2nd ed. Rome: Pontifical Biblical Institute, 1970.

Gardiner, A. H. *Egyptian Hieratic Texts.* Leipzig: J. C. Hinrichs, 1911.

Garr, W. R. "*ay > a in Targum Onqelos," *JAOS* (forthcoming).

_____. *Dialect Geography of Syria-Palestine, 1000–586 B.C.E.* Philadelphia: University of Pennsylvania Press, 1985.

Gaster, T. H. "Psalm 29," *JQR* 37 (1946–1947) 55–65.

_____. "Psalm 42: 8," *JBL* 73 (1954) 237–38.

_____. "Psalm 45," *JBL* 74 (1955) 239–51.

_____. *Thespis.* New York: Gordian Press, 1975.

Gese, H. "Psalm 50 und das alttestamentliche Gesetzesverständnis," *Rechtfertigung: Festschrift für Ernst Käsemann zum 70. Geburtstag.*

Eds. J. Friedrich, W. Pöhlmann, and P. Stuhlmacher. Tübingen: J. C. B. Mohr, 1976. Pp. 57–77.

Gevirtz, S. "Asher in the Blessing of Jacob (Genesis xlix 20)," *VT* 37 (1987) 154–63.

_____. "Of Syntax and Style in the 'Late Biblical Hebrew'—'Old Canaanite' Connection," *JANES* 18 (1986) 25–29.

_____. "On the Etymology of the Phoenician Particle אֹש," *JNES* 16 (1957) 124–27.

Ginsberg, H. L. *The Israelian Heritage of Judaism.* New York: Jewish Theological Seminary, 1982.

_____. *Kitve ʾUgarit.* Jerusalem: Bialik, 1936.

_____. *The Legend of King Keret.* BASORSS 2–3. New Haven: American Schools of Oriental Research, 1946.

_____. "The Northwest Semitic Languages, in *Patriarchs.* World History of the Jewish People. Ed. B. Mazar. New Brunswick: Rutgers University Press, 1970. Pp. 102–24, 293.

_____. "A Phoenician Hymn in the Psalter," in *Atti del XIX Congresso Internazionale degli Orientalisti (Roma 1935).* Rome: G. Bardi, 1938. Pp. 472–476.

_____. "A Strand in the Cord of Hebraic Hymnody," *Eretz-Israel* 9 (W. F. Albright Volume) (1969) 45–50.

Gonzalez, A. "Le psaume lxxxii," *VT* 13 (1963) 293–309.

Gordis, R. *The Book of Job.* New York: Jewish Theological Seminary, 1978.

_____. "Psalm 9–10—A Textual and Exegetical Study," *JQR* 48 (1958) 104–22.

_____. "Was Koheleth a Phoenician?" *JBL* 74 (1955) 103–14.

Gordon, C. H. *The Ancient Near East.* New York: Norton, 1965.

_____. "New Directions," *BASP* 15 (Naphtali Lewis Festschrift) (1978) 59–66.

_____. "North Israelite Influence on Postexilic Hebrew," *IEJ* 5 (1955) 85–88.

_____. "The Poetic Literature of Ugarit," *Orientalia* 12 (1943) 31–75.

_____. *Ugaritic Textbook.* AnOr 38. Rome: Pontifical Biblical Institute, 1967.

Goulder, M. D. *The Psalms of the Sons of Korah.* JSOTSS 20. Sheffield: JSOT Press, 1982.

Gray, J. *The Krt Text in the Literature of Ras Shamra.* Leiden: E. J. Brill, 1964.

Greenberg, J. H. "Internal *a*-Plurals in Afroasiatic (Hamito-Semitic)," in *Afrikanistische Studien.* Ed. J. Lukas. Berlin: Akademie Verlag, 1955. Pp. 198–204.

Greenberg, M. "Mizmor 140," *Eretz-Israel* 14 (H. L. Ginsberg Volume) (1978) 88–99.

Greenfield, J. C. "Aramaic Studies and the Bible," in *Congress Volume Vienna 1980.* SVT 32. Ed. J. A. Emerton. Leiden: E. J. Brill, 1981. Pp. 110–30.

_____. "The 'Periphrastic Imperative' in Aramaic and Hebrew," *IEJ* 19 (1969) 199–210.

_____. "Review of J. Hoftijzer and G. van der Kooij, *Aramaic Texts from Deir ʿAlla,*" *JSS* 25 (1980) 248–52.

Greenspahn, F. E. *Hapax Legomena in Biblical Hebrew.* SBLDS 74. Chico, CA: Scholars Press, 1984.

Gröndahl, F. *Die Personennamen der Texte aus Ugarit.* Rome: Pontifical Biblical Institute, 1967.

Gualandi, D. "Salmo 141 (140)," *RBI* 6 (1958) 219–23.

Gunkel, H. "Psalm 133," in *Karl Budde zum siebzigsten Geburtstag.* Ed. K. Marti. BZAW 34. Giessen: Alfred Töpelmann, 1920. Pp. 69–74.

_____. *Die Psalmen.* HKAT. Göttingen: Vandenhoeck & Ruprecht, 1926.

Hackett, J. A. *The Balaam Text from Deir ʿAllā.* HSM 31. Chico, CA: Scholars Press, 1980.

Halpern, B. "Dialect Distribution in Canaan and the Deir ʿAlla Inscriptions," in *"Working With No Data": Semitic and Egyptian Studies Presented to Thomas O. Lambdin.* Ed. D. M. Golomb. Winona Lake, IN: Eisenbrauns, 1987. Pp. 119–39.

Hanson, R. S. *Tyrian Influence in the Upper Galilee.* Cambridge, MA: American Schools of Oriental Research, 1980.

Harris, Z. *A Grammar of the Phoenician Language.* AOS 8. New Haven, CT: American Oriental Society, 1936.

Heinemann, H. "The Date of Psalm 80," *JQR* 40 (1949–50) 297–302.

Held, M. "Pits and Pitfalls in Akkadian and Biblical Hebrew," *JANES* 5 (1973) 173–90.

Hestrin, R., *et al. Ketuvot Mesaprot.* Jerusalem: Israel Museum, 1973.

Hidal, S. "Some Reflections on Deuteronomy 32," *ASTI* 11 (1977–78) 15–21.

Hill, D. "'Son of Man' in Psalm 80 v. 17," *NT* 15 (1973) 261–69.

Hillers, D. "Ritual Procession of the Ark and Ps 132," *CBQ* 30 (1968) 48–55.

Hofbauer, J. "Psalm 77/78, ein 'politisch Lied'," *ZKT* 89 (1967) 41–50.

Huffmon, H. B. *Amorite Personal Names in the Mari Texts.* Baltimore: Johns Hopkins Press, 1965.

Hurvitz, A. *Beyn Lashon le-Lashon.* Jerusalem: Bialik, 1972.

_____. "Ha-Lashon ha-ʿIvrit ba-Tequfa ha-Parsit," in *Shivat Ṣiyyon—Yeme Shilton Paras.* Ha-Historiya shel ʿAm Yisraʾel. Jerusalem: Alexander Peli, 1983. 210–23, 306–9.

_____. "Linguistic Criteria for Dating Problematic Biblical Texts," *Hebrew Abstracts* 14 (1973) 74–79.

_____. *A Linguistic Study of the Relationship Between the Priestly Source and the Book of Ezekiel.* Paris: J. Gabalda, 1982.

_____, ed. *Miqraʾa be-Ḥeqer Leshon ha-Miqraʾ.* Liquṭe Tarbiz 3. Jerusalem: Magnes, 1982–83.

Hyatt, J. P. "A Note on *yiwwadaʿ* in Ps. 74:5," *AJSL* 58 (1941) 99–100.

Irsigler, H. *Psalm 73—Monolog eines Weisen.* St. Ottilien: EOS Verlag, 1984.

Japhet, S. "People and Land in the Restoration Period," in *Das Land Israel in biblischer Zeit.* Ed. G. Strecker. Göttingen: Vandenhoeck & Ruprecht, 1983. Pp. 103–125.

Jastrow, M. *A Dictionary of the Targumim, the Talmud Babli and Yerushalmi, and the Midrashic Literature.* 2 vols. London: Luzac, 1903.

Jefferson, H. G. "Psalm lxxviii," *VT* 13 (1963) 87–91.

Jirku, A. "Doppelte Überlieferungen im Mythus und im Epos von Ugarit?" *ZDMG* 110 (1960) 20–25.

Joüon, P. *Grammaire de l'hébreu biblique.* Rome: Pontifical Biblical Institute, 1923.

Junker, H. "Unité, composition et genre littéraire des psaumes IX et X," *RB* 60 (1953) 161–69.

Kaufman, S. A. "The Classification of the North West Semitic Dialects of the Biblical Period and Some Implications Thereof," in *Proceedings of the Ninth World Congress of Jewish Studies.* Panel Sessions:

Hebrew and Aramaic Languages. Jerusalem: World Union of Jewish Studies, 1988. Pp. 41–57.

Kautzsch, E. *Die Aramaismen im Alten Testament.* Halle: M. Niemeyer, 1902.

_____. *Gesenius' Hebrew Grammar.* Trans. A. E. Cowley. Oxford: Clarendon Press, 1910.

King, E. G. "On the Text of Psalms XIV and LIII," *Hebraica* 2 (1885–86) 237–39.

King, P. J. *A Study of Psalm 45 (44).* Ph.D. dissertation, Pontificia Universitas Lateranensis. Rome, 1959.

Kloos, C. *YHWH's Combat with the Sea.* Leiden: E. J. Brill, 1986.

Koehler, L., and W. Baumgartner, *Lexicon in Veteris Testamenti libros.* Leiden: E. J. Brill, 1985.

Kraus, H.-J. *Psalmen.* 2 vols. Neukirchen: Neukirchener Verlag, 1960.

Krinetzki, P. L. "Zur Poetik Exegese von Ps 48," *BZ* 4 (1960) 70–97.

Kruse, H. "Psalm cxxxii and the Royal Zion Festival," *VT* 33 (1983) 279–97.

_____. "Two Hidden Comparatives: Observations on Hebrew Style," *JSS* 5 (1960) 333–47.

Kutscher, E. Y. "Be-Shuley ha-Millon ha-Miqraʾi," *Leshonenu* 32 (1967–68) 343–46.

_____. "Ha-Śafa ha-ʿIvrit u-Venot Livyata be-Meshek ha-Dorot," *Hadoar* 47 (1968–69) 507–9.

_____. *Hebrew and Aramaic Studies.* Jerusalem: Magnes, 1977.

_____. *A History of the Hebrew Language.* Jerusalem: Magnes, 1982.

_____. "Nišmedû bĕʿên dôr, hāyû dōmen lāʾădāmāh (Tehillim 83,11)," *Yediʿot ha-Ḥevra ha-ʿIvrit le-Ḥaqirat ʾEreṣ Yiśraʾel ve-ʿAtiqoteha* 2 (1934–35) 40–42.

Lahav, M. "Mihu *hāʾăšûrî* (Shemuʾel Bet 2,9) ve-ʾaššûr(Tehillim 83,9)," *Beth Miqra* 28 (1983) 111–12.

Le Mat, L. A. F. *Textual Criticism and Exegesis of Psalm XXXVI.* Utrecht: Kemink & Zoon, 1957.

Leveen, J. "Psalm X: A Reconstruction," *JTS* 45 (1944) 16–21.

_____. "Textual Problems in the Psalms," *VT* 21 (1971) 48–58.

Levi, J. *Die Inkongruenz im biblischen Hebräisch.* Wiesbaden: Otto Harrassowitz, 1987.

Liebschutz, N. "An Interpretation of Psalm 74," *ASJL* 40 (1924) 284–87.

Lindblom, J. "Erwägungen zu Psalm xvi," *VT* 24 (1974) 187–95.

Liverani, M. "Elementi innovativi nell'Ugaritico non letterario," *Atti della Accademia nazionale dei Lince, Rendiconti della Classe di scienze morali, storiche e filologiche.* Series VIII, Vol. 19, No. 5–6 (1964) 173–91.

Loewenstamm, S. E. "Bilʿam," *EM* 2 (1973) 133–34.

_____. "ʿēdût bîhôsēp," *Eretz-Israel* 5 (Benjamin Mazar Volume) (1958) 80–82.

Lohfink, N. "Deuteronomy," in *Interpreter's Dictionary of the Bible.* Supplementary Volume. Ed. K. Crim. Nashville, TN: Abingdon, 1976. Pp. 229–32.

Loretz, O. *Psalm 29: Kanaanäische El- und Baaltraditionen in jüdischer Sicht.* UBL 2. Soest: CIS-Verlag, 1984.

_____. *Die Psalmen: Beitrag der Ugarit-Texte zum Verständnis von Kolometrie und Textologie der Psalmen.* 2 vols. AOAT 207. Neukirchen-Vluyn: Neukirchener Verlag, 1979.

_____. "Psalmenstudien," *UF* 3 (1971) 101–15.

Machinist, P. "Assyria and Its Image in the First Isaiah," *JAOS* 103 (1983) 719–37.

Mannati, M. "Les adorateurs de Môt dans le psaume lxxiii," *VT* 22 (1972) 420–25.

_____. "Le psaume 50 est-il un *rîb*?" *Semitica* 23 (1973) 27–49.

Margulis, B. "The Canaanite Origin of Psalm 29 Reconsidered," *Biblica* 51 (1970) 332–48.

Mazar, B. "Qiryat Yeʿarim," *EM* 7 (1976) 270–72.

Mazar, B., A. Biran, M. Dothan, and I. Dunayevsky, "ʿEin Gev Excavations in 1961," *IEJ* 14 (1964) 1–49.

McCarter, P. K. *I Samuel.* AB 8. Garden City, NY: Doubleday, 1980.

_____. *II Samuel.* AB 9. Garden City, NY: Doubleday, 1984.

Melamed, E. Z. "Shnayim shehem ʾeḥad (*hen dia duoin*) ba-Miqraʾ," *Tarbiz* 16 (1944–45) 173–89.

Miller, J. M. "The Korahites of Southern Judah," *CBQ* 32 (1970) 58–68.

Morag, S. "ʿIyyunim be-Yaḥase Mashmaʿot," *Eretz-Israel* 14 (H. L. Ginsberg Volume) (1978) 137–47.

_____. "On the Historical Validity of the Vocalization of Biblical Hebrew," *JAOS* 94 (1974) 307–15.

_____. "Rovde Qadmut: ʿIyyunim Leshoniyim be-Mishle Bilʿam," *Tarbiz* 50 (1980–81) 1–24.

Moran, W. L. "The Hebrew Language in its Northwest Semitic Background," in *The Bible and the Ancient Near East: Essays in Honor of William Foxwell Albright*. Ed. G. E. Wright. Garden City, NY: Doubleday, 1961. Pp. 54–72.

_____. "*taqtul*—Third Masculine Singular?" Biblica 45 (1964) 80–82.

Morgenstern, J. "The Mythological Background of Psalm 82," *HUCA* 14 (1939) 29–126.

_____. "Psalm 48," *HUCA* 16 (1943) 1–95.

Mulder, J. S. M. *Studies on Psalm 45*. Ph.D. dissertation, Katholieke Universiteit te Nijmegen. Nijmegen, 1972.

Nasuti, H. P. *Tradition History and the Psalms of Asaph*. SBLDS 88. Atlanta: Scholars Press, 1988.

Naveh, J. "Review of J. Hoftijzer and G. van der Kooij, *Aramaic Texts from Deir ʿAlla*," *IEJ* 29 (1979) 133–36.

Nielsen, E. "Historical Perspectives and Geographical Horizons: On the Question of North-Israelite Elements in Deuteronomy," *ASTI* 11 (1977–78) 77–89.

Norin, S. "Ps. 133. Zusammenhang und Datierung," *ASTI* 11 (1977–78) 90–95.

Nowack, W. *Richter, Ruth, und Bucher Samuelis*. HKAT. Göttingen: Vandenhoeck & Ruprecht, 1902.

O'Callaghan, R. T. "A Note on the Canaanite Background of Psalm 82," *CBQ* 15 (1953) 311–14.

Olivier, J. P. J. "The Sceptre of Justice and Ps. 45:7b," *JNSL* 7 (1979) 45–54.

Orlinsky, H. M. "The Origins of the Kethib-Qere System: A New Approach," in *Congress Volume Oxford 1959*. SVT 7. Leiden: E. J. Brill, 1960. 184–92.

_____. "Prolegomenon," in C. D. Ginsburg. *Introduction to the Massoretico-Critical Edition of the Hebrew Bible*. New York: Ktav, 1966. Pp. I-XLV.

Parisot, J. "Psaumes de la captivité," *RB* 4 (1895) 572–78.

Payne Smith, J. *A Compendious Syriac Dictionary*. Oxford: Clarendon Press, 1903.

Peters, J. "A Jerusalem Processional," *JPOS* 1 (1920) 36–41.

_____. *The Psalms as Liturgies*. New York: Macmillan, 1922.

Pitard, W. T. *Ancient Damascus*. Winona Lake, IN: Eisenbrauns, 1987.

van der Ploeg, J. "Notes sur le Psaume xlix," in *Studies on Psalms*. OTS 13. Leiden: E. J. Brill, 1963. Pp. 137–72.

Podechard, E. "Notes sur les psaumes," *RB* 32 (1923) 238–52.

_____. "Notes sur les Psaumes: Psaume XLIX," *RB* 31 (1922) 5–19.

Polzin, R. *Late Biblical Hebrew: Toward an Historical Typology of Biblical Hebrew Prose*. HSM 12. Missoia, MT: Scholars Press, 1976.

Pope, M. H. *Job*. AB 15. Garden City, NY: Doubleday, 1973.

_____. "A Little Soul-Searching," *Maarav* 1 (1978) 25–31.

_____. *Song of Songs*. AB 7C. Garden City, NY: Doubleday, 1977.

Power, E. "Ṣion or Si'on in Psalm 133 (Vulg 132)," *Biblica* 3 (1922) 342–49.

Pritchard, J. B. *Ancient Near Eastern Texts Relating to the Old Testament*. Princeton: Princeton University Press, 1969.

Procksch, O. *Das nordhebräische Sagenbuch, Die Elohimquelle*. Leipzig: J. C. Hinrichs, 1906.

Rabin, C. "The Emergence of Classical Hebrew," in *The Age of the Monarchies: Culture and Society*. World History of the Jewish People. Ed. A. Malamat. Jerusalem: Masada Press, 1979. Pp. 71–78, 293–95.

_____. "Leshonam shel ʿAmos ve-Hosheaʿ," in *ʿIyyunim be-Sefer Tre-ʿAsar*. Ed. B. Z. Luria. Jerusalem: Kiryath Sepher, 1981. Pp. 117–36.

Rainey, A. F. "The Soldier-Scribe in *Papyrus Anastasi I*," *JNES* 26 (1967) 58–60.

Ratner, R. J. *Gender Problems in Biblical Hebrew*. Ph.D. dissertation, Hebrew Union College-Jewish Institute of Religion. Cincinnati, 1983.

Reider, J. "Contributions to the Hebrew Lexicon," *ZAW* 53 (1935) 270–77.

_____. "Miscellanea Hebraica," *JJS* 3 (1952) 78–86.

Rendsburg, G. A. "Additional Notes on 'The Last Words of David' (2 Sam. 23, 1–7)," *Biblica* 70 (1989) 403–8.

_____. "The Ammonite Phoneme /T̤/," *BASOR* 269 (1988) 73–79.

_____. *Diglossia in Ancient Hebrew*. AOS. Ann Arbor, MI: American Oriental Society, 1990.

_____. "The Galilean Background of Mishnaic Hebrew," in *Proceedings of the First International Conference on Galilean Studies in Late Antiquity*. Ed. L. Levine. Jerusalem, forthcoming.

_____. "Janus Parallelism in Gen 49:26," *JBL* 99 (1980) 291–93.

_____. "Monophthongization of *aw/ay* > *ā* in Eblaite and in Northwest Semitic," in *Eblaitica: Essays on the Ebla Archives and Eblaite Language*. Vol. 2. Eds. C. H. Gordon and G. A. Rendsburg. Winona Lake, IN: Eisenbrauns, 1990. Pp. 91–126.

_____. "More on Hebrew *Šibbōlet*," *JSS* 33 (1988) 255–58.

_____. "Morphological Evidence for Regional Dialects in Ancient Hebrew," in *Linguistics and Biblical Hebrew*. Ed. W. Bodine. Winona Lake, IN: Eisenbrauns, forthcoming,

_____. "The Northern Origin of 'The Last Words of David' (2 Sam. 23, 1–7)," *Biblica* 69 (1988) 113–21.

_____. "A Reconstruction of Moabite-Israelite History," *JANES* 13 (1981) 67–73.

Rinaldi, G. "Nota," *Bibbia e Oriente*. 22 (1980) 124.

Ringgren, H. "Einige Bemerkungen zum lxxiii. Psalm," *VT* 3 (1953) 265–72.

Robertson, D. A. *Linguistic Evidence in Dating Early Hebrew Poetry*. SBLDS 3. Missoula, MT: Society of Biblical Literature, 1972.

Robinson, A. "Do Ephrathah and Jaar Really Appear in Psalm 132:6?" *ZAW* 86 (1974) 220–22.

_____. "The Meaning of *ri* and the Dubiety of the Form *harre* and Its Variants," *VT* 24 (1974) 500–4.

_____. "A Possible Solution to the Problem of Psalm 74:5," *ZAW* 89 (1977) 120–21.

_____. "Three Suggested Interpretations in Ps. lxxxiv," *VT* 24 (1974) 378–81.

_____. "Zion and *Saphon* in Psalm XLVIII 3," *VT* 24 (1974) 118–23.

Robinson, F. C. "Some Aspects of the *Maldon* Poet's Artistry," *Journal of English and Germanic Philology* 75 (1976) 25–40.

Roifer (Rofé), A. *"Yāṣāʾ mēḥēleb ʿēnēmô,"* *Tarbiz* 32 (1962–63) 109–13.

_____. "Siyyumo shel Tehillim Pereq 80," *Tarbiz* 29 (1959–60) 113–24.

Rosenthal, F. *A Grammar of Biblical Aramaic.* Wiesbaden: Otto Harrassowitz, 1974.

Ross, J. F. "Psalm 73," in *Israelite Wisdom: Theological and Literary Essays in Honor of Samuel Terrien.* Eds. J. G. Gammie, W. A. Brueggemann, W. L. Humphreys, and J. M. Ward. New York: Union Theological Seminary, 1978. Pp. 161–75.

Rossell, W. H. *A Handbook of Aramaic Magical Texts.* Ringwood Borough, NJ: Shelton College, 1955.

Sarna, N. M. "The Divine Title ʾabhîr yaʿăqôbh," in *Essays on the Occasion of the Seventieth Anniversary of Dropsie University.* Eds. A. I. Katsh and L. Nemoy. Philadelphia: Dropsie University, 1979. 389–96.

_____. "The Interchange of the Prepositions *Beth* and *Min* in Biblical Hebrew," *JBL* 78 (1959) 310–16.

_____. "The Mythological Background of Job 18," *JBL* 82 (1963) 315–18.

_____. "Psalm 89: A Study in Inner Biblical Exegesis," in *Biblical and Other Studies.* Ed. A. Altmann. Cambridge, MA: Harvard University Press, 1963. Pp. 29–46.

Schreiner, J. *Zion-Jerusalem Jahwes Königssitz.* Munich: Kösel-Verlag, 1963.

Schuttermayr, G. "Ambivalenz und Aspektdifferenz: Bemerkungen zu den hebräischen Präpositionen *b, l,* und *mn*," *BZ* 15 (1971) 29–51.

_____. *Psalm 9–10: Studien zur Textkritik und Übersetzung.* St. Ottilien: EOS Verlag, 1985.

Scott, R. B. Y. *Proverbs-Ecclesiastes.* AB 18. Garden City, NY: Doubleday, 1965.

Segal, M. H. (M. Z.) *Diqduq Leshon ha-Mishna.* Tel-Aviv: Dvir, 1936.

_____. *A Grammar of Mishnaic Hebrew.* Oxford: Clarendon Press, 1927.

Segert, S. *Altaramäische Grammatik.* Leipzig: VEB Verlag, 1975.

Seybold, K. "Psalm lviii. Ein Lösungsversuch," *VT* 30 (1980) 53–66.

_____. "Die Redaktion der Wallfahrtspsalmen," *ZAW* 91 (1979) 246–68.

Simpson, W. G. "Some Egyptian Light on a Translation Problem in Psalm X," *VT* 19 (1969) 128–31.

Sivan, D. *Grammatical Analysis and Glossary of the Northwest Semitic Vocables in Akkadian Texts of the 15th-13th C. B.C. from Canaan and Syria.* AOAT 214. Neukirchen-Vluyn: Neukirchener Verlag, 1984.

Steiner, R. C. *The Case for Fricative-Laterals in Proto-Semitic.* AOS. New Haven: American Oriental Society, 1977.

Stuhlmueller, C. "Psalms," in *Harper's Bible Commentary.* Ed. J. L. Mays. San Francisco: Harper & Row, 1988. Pp. 433–94.

Sturtevant, E. H. *An Introduction to Linguistic Science.* New Haven: Yale University Press, 1947.

Tomback, R. S. *A Comparative Semitic Lexicon of the Phoenician and Punic Languages.* SBLDS 32. Missoula, MT: Scholars Press, 1978.

Torrey, C. C. "The Archetype of Psalms 14 and 53," *JBL* 46 (1927) 186–92.

Tournay, R. J. "Les affinités du Ps. xlv avec le Cantique des Cantiques et leurs interprétation messianique," in *Congress Volume Bonn 1962.* SVT 9. Leiden: E. J. Brill, 1963. Pp. 168–212.

_____. "Notes sur les psaumes," *RB* 79 (1972) 39–58.

_____. "Le Psaume XXXVI: Structure et Doctrine," *RB* 90 (1983) 5–22.

_____. "Le psaume cxli," *VT* 9 (1959) 58–64.

_____. "Psaume CXLI: Nouvelle interprétation," *RB* 90 (1983) 321–33.

_____. "Les psaumes complexes," *RB* 54 (1947) 521–42.

Tsevat, M. "God and the Gods in Assembly," *HUCA* 40–41 (1969–70) 123–37.

_____. *The Meaning of the Book of Job and Other Biblical Studies.* New York: Ktav, 1980.

_____. *A Study of the Language of the Biblical Psalms.* JBLMS 9. Philadelphia: Society of Biblical Literature, 1955.

Tur-Sinai, N. H. "ʾAramit: Hashpaʿat ha-ʾAramit ʿal ha-ʿIvrit shel ha-Miqraʾ," *EM* 1 (1985) 593–95.

_____. *The Book of Job.* Jerusalem: Kiryath Sepher, 1957.

Ullendorff, E. "The Contribution of South Semitics to Hebrew Lexicography," *VT* 6 (1956) 190–98.

_____. *Is Biblical Hebrew a Language?* Wiesbaden: Otto Harrassowitz, 1977.

Vaccari, A. "Note critiche ed esegetiche," *Biblica* 28 (1947) 394–406.

Volz, P. "Psalm 49," *ZAW* 55 (1937) 235–64.

Wagner, M. *Die lexicalischen und grammatikalischen Aramaismen im alttestmentlichen Hebräisch*. BZAW 96. Berlin: Alfred Töpelmann, 1966.

Watson, W. G. E. *Classical Hebrew Poetry: A Guide to its Techniques*. JSOTSS 26. Sheffield: JSOT Press, 1984.

Weiser, A. *The Psalms*. OTL. Philadelphia: Westminster, 1962.

Weiss, M. *The Bible From Within: The Method of Total Interpretation*. Jerusalem: Magnes, 1984.

Weiss, R. "Textual Notes," *Textus* 6 (1968) 127–31.

Weissblit, S. "Tehillim Mizmor 14 ve-ha-Maqbil Lo 53," *Beth Miqra* 29 (1983–84) 133–38.

Welch, A. C. "The Source of Nehemiah IX," *ZAW* 47 (1929) 130–37.

Widengren, G. "Review of M. Seligson, *The Meaning of* npš mt *in the Old Testament*," *VT* 4 (1954) 97–102.

Wiener, H. M. "The Historical Background of Psalm lxxxiii," *JPOS* 8 (1928) 180–86.

Willesen, F. "The Cultic Situation of Psalm lxxiv," *VT* 2 (1952) 289–306.

Wilson, R. R. *Prophecy and Society in Ancient Israel*. Philadelphia: Fortress, 1980.

Yellin, D. "Emek Ha-Bakha: Bekhaim," *JPOS* 3 (1923) 191–92.

Zevit, Z. "Psalms on the Poetic Precipice," *HAR* 10 (1986) 351–66.

_____. "The So-called Interchangeability of the Prepositions *b*, *l*, and *m(n)* in Northwest Semitic," *JANES* 7 (1975) 105–11.

Zorell, F. "Kritisches zu einigen Psalmversen," *Biblica* 7 (1926) 311–20.

_____. "Psalm 80. Gebet für das Volk Gottes," *BZ* 15 (1921) 122–24.

_____. "Zu Ps 12,9; 76,6," *Biblica* 10 (1929) 100.

Zurro, E. "Disemia de *brḥ* y paralelismo bifronte en Job 9,25," *Biblica* 62 (1981) 546–47.

Index of Biblical Passages

See also Index of Subjects for individual biblical books.

INDEX OF SCHOLARS CITED

INDEX OF SUBJECTS

General terms (Canaanite, Hebrew, Northwest Semitic, etc.) and commonly occurring terms (Jerusalem, Judahite Hebrew, Israelian Hebrew, etc.) are not indexed.